# MY WAR STORY

The WWII Memoir of Private
Bill Lowcock

2/19th Battalion A.I.F.

# JOSHUA LOWCOCK

www.JoshuaLowcock.com

# DEDICATION

This book would not have been possible without the support of my wife and son. Thank you both for your patience, support, and encouragement throughout the process—and in everything that I undertake.

A special thank you to Lt. Col Peter Winstanley OAM RFD (Retired) JP for maintaining the 'Prisoners of War of Japan' website and helping to preserve Bill Lowcock's story.

I am indebted to the Australian War Memorial Canberra and their digital archives, particularly for the library of copyright free images. If you appreciate the images as I did, please donate to the Australian War Memorial.

Most importantly, I want to thank and acknowledge Private William (Bill) Mackenzie Lowcock who sacrificed so much for us all, and who had the foresight to ensure there was a meticulous record of his experience.

# TABLE OF CONTENTS

# FOREWORD

———————— ◆ ◇ ◆ ————————

Our lessons about Australia's participation in World War I and World War II still rank among my strongest memories from school in Australia. As students, in the lead up to each ANZAC Day on April 25th, we were taught about the "ANZAC Spirit" and the importance of honouring and remembering the service of all those who had served for our country and for us.

Despite these lessons, despite marching in ANZAC parades as a boy scout and visiting the Australian War Memorial in Canberra, I had absolutely no idea about my second cousin Private William (Bill) Lowcock, and about his service and experience as a Prisoner of War (POW).

Unfortunately, I wouldn't come to learn of Bill until much later in life and well after Bill's passing, when an interest in unearthing lost family history connected the dots.

Then, it seemed amiss, in honouring all the men whose lives had been lost, I had never really 'seen' Bill before, and yet here he was in my very own family, his story begging to be told.

Having discovered that he had been captured by the Japanese and forced to work on the infamous Thai-Burma Railway, I wanted to ensure that his memory was honoured.

Bill's story is honest, candid, sometimes humorous—and, at even the worst of times, without any sense of despair. His survival is a testament to what is unique about the ANZAC spirit and looking after your mates.

And what's even better is that he told it himself, in diarised notes I was honoured to be able to resurrect and present to you in this book.

For over a year, I have worked to research, edit, structure, check, annotate, and even illustrate Bill's story so that it can be permanently preserved, shared, and understood by future generations.

This is done out of respect not only for Bill, but also for all those brave men who served.

I share all of this as it's not my intention to claim Bill Lowcock as an immediate family member or someone that I knew personally. This book is intended to respectfully honour his memory and as the "Ode to the Fallen" which every Australian child recites on ANZAC Day instructs us.

*'At the going down of the sun and in the morning,*
*we will remember them.*
*Lest we forget.'*

# PREFACE

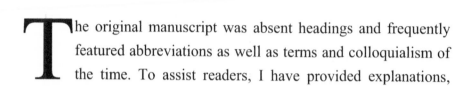

The original manuscript was absent headings and frequently featured abbreviations as well as terms and colloquialism of the time. To assist readers, I have provided explanations, translations and/or footnotes.

*(Italicized text)* in parentheses represents notes or commentary added to provide clarity and to ensure the reader can follow the story.

Footnotes are given for additional information where necessary or useful, either for historical context or where there is a detail that might enhance the understanding of the story.

Photographs are sourced from the Australia War Memorial (AWM) and include the AWM index number. Photos may not reflect the exact date or time in the story and are provided for context and as a visual aid, to bring Bill's story to life.

I have never spoken about my wartime experiences to anybody in civilian life. If anyone wants to read it, well that's great.

BILL LOWCOCK

*Figure 1: William (Bill) Mackenzie Lowcock. NX10682*
*Inscribed: "To Mavis, with love from Bill x" (AWM P12658)*

# PRELUDE TO WAR

———————— ◆ ◇ ◆ ————————

The best place to start any memoir, of course, is at the beginning. I joined the militia in 1936 just after my sixteenth birthday. I joined the New South Wales Scottish Regiment[1], the 30th battalion. They were allied with the Black Watch[2], wore the Black Watch uniform—a very proud unit they were. I was underage at sixteen but I was fortunate that one of the platoon commanders was Bruff Bond, Lieutenant, and he had been at Kings School with my brother Boyce; a little bit of influence was extended and I got in as a cadet.

Twelve months later, I was accepted as a Private and attended weekly drills at the drill hall, right next to the old Garrison Church at Millers Point. We went on a month's camp every year, usually to Rutherford or Greta and nothing really exciting happened until just before the outbreak of World War II on the 3rd of September 1939.

A fortnight before then, a few us were warned to be ready to move at twelve hours' notice. We didn't know what for or what was going on, but when war was declared on September 3, news came around the streets—about ten o'clock at night, it was.

---

[1] At the time, the Scottish Regiment was a hybrid Home Guard and the Army Reserve.
[2] The Black Watch is an infantry battalion with its roots in the Royal Regiment of Scotland.

Newspapers were being delivered by local newsagents—'War Has Been Declared'. And about half an hour later, I got a phone call to report to the drill hall tomorrow morning, 0900 hours.

The next morning, Mum had all the gear ready and I saddled up the whole works, kit bag and all, and off I went to the drill hall. I felt a bit of a fool going across on the ferry because the war was only a day old and here I was in uniform.

Where the hell was I going?

Anyway, we finished up being trucked down to Glebe where the Purr Pull Company[3] had a petrol depot. I don't know how many million gallons there were, but there were half a dozen enormous tanks on the waterfront there.

Our job was to guard the tanks, to keep the saboteurs out. Nothing terribly exciting happened there except we did catch one saboteur there late one night. A fellow walking around with a blooming great spanner in his hand and we heard him while we were policing, and it turned out he was bent on opening a valve somewhere and striking a match.

Had that happened, of course, half of Glebe would have burned.

Another time, I was on duty on a walkway overlooking the water when a small putt-putt launch (*motorized small dinghy*) approached. I called a challenge twice and it did not stop, so I put a round of .303 into the water about six feet from its bow.

Immediately, the engine stopped and one of two men on board called out, "Don't shoot!" It turned out they were the water police.

---

[3] Purr Pull was the brand name of fuel/gasoline used by Independent Oil Industries of Sydney

We spent about a month there and then it was the Sergeant, myself and half a dozen other blokes were transferred up to Newcastle, to Stockton where we were guarding the water pipe. Newcastle's water came underneath the harbour in an enormous great water pipe about three feet across, and we were stationed on the southern end of that to make sure nobody blew it up.

Again, nothing terribly exciting, but a cushy (*easy*) job. We spent about a month there and then I went back to work for the Bank of New South Wales[4].

---

[4] The Bank of New South Wales now trades as Westpac.

# WAR IS DECLARED

———————— ◆ ◇ ◆ ————————

In about January 1940, John Moysey—an old school friend of mine—and I decided we would join the Air Force. We went down to the Air Force Recruiting Depot at Woolloomooloo, and lined up, and together with probably another hundred blokes there, we did an aptitude test.

We both passed that, as all they wanted to find out was if you could read and write and add up two and two. John, unfortunately, had very bad eyesight and he got thrown out there. He didn't get past the aptitude test. But I did and I was given the papers and told, "Take these back, get your father to sign them and you're in."

Well, I went home, and my father refused to sign the papers.

I have no doubt he had his very good reasons, but I never forgave him for that, and it caused a lasting rift in my relationship with my father, which was unfortunate.

For the next eighteen months, there was nothing left to do but soldier on with the 30th. We spent a lot of time in camp. We trained the universal trainees—the eighteen-year-olds who were conscripted in. Nothing exciting happening there.

We were at Ingleburn in May 1941 and on the 23rd of May, I got leave to go down and join the AIF (*Australian Imperial Force[5]*). I turned twenty-one on 24th May.

---

[5] The AIF, Australian Imperial Force, also known as the 2nd AIF, active from 1939-1947.

I went down to the Sydney Showgrounds and signed up, signed all the papers, took the oath and they gave me a uniform and told me to go to the pig pens there and find somewhere to sleep. "The cookhouse is down the road. Get some tucker and report back in the morning."

The bloke next to me in the next pig pen—or, we shared one pen, I think—was a fellow named Bob Britton, known as Bluey Britton or Blue. We became good mates from then on, and his number was the next number to mine. NX 10682 was mine and he was NX 10683[6] or NX 10681[7], I'm not sure which. But the next day, we shipped off to Dubbo.

Bob Britton was quite a character. He lived in Ultimo and had been in the Navy for several years until apparently, the Navy decided they didn't want him anymore and he was discharged. A bit of a wild lad, Blue loved his drink and he was incredibly strong. We used to wrestle in fun, and I could never beat him. We got on very well.

Blue was not very bright, and Dubbo was a wide-open wild town for the army.

There was a pub on every corner and Friday nights, if we could get leave, we would all hop on the bus into town and the first port of call was the Greeks in Macquarie Street where we had a big plate of steak and eggs. Then down to the pub.

There was a good pub right opposite the railway station. We would have a few beers there and the Blue would go and play the Under and Overs (*gambling on sports scores)*, the Crown and Anchor (*a gambling game played with dice)* or the SWY game (*two up, a gambling game played with coins)* that was running just across the street. In those days in New South Wales, the pubs closed at six, or

---

[6] Robert Samuel Britton NX10679, which is close to the number recalled by Bill.
[7] NX 10681 is Private Mervyn Leo Morris 11.9.22 - 11.9.81.

they should have done. The pubs in Dubbo never seemed to close and you could always walk in and get a drink almost any time you liked and the gambling joint was quite open; nobody bothered to lock the doors, no passwords to get in, you just got in and that was it.

Blue's problem was that he had no idea he was a compulsive gambler and he had no idea about handling his money. We were being paid five bob (*slang for shilling, a unit of currency*) a day and if he wasn't careful, by the end of the Friday night, he would have nothing left. I used to take half his pay and keep it for him and when he went broke on Friday night, we would go back to camp and then he would have a bit of money to spend for the rest of the week.

# BASIC TRAINING

———————— ◆ ◇ ◆ ————————

D ubbo was a Basic Training Camp. Raw recruits came in and they were trained, and the section I was in was a hell of a big camp. The section was sending recruits to the 2/33rd Battalion[8]; I think that was 7th division. I was there for about a month or so and in that time, three drafts went off to the Middle East without me. The problem was, with my militia training, they were short of instructors and they made me an instructor. This didn't give me much joy at all.

Eventually, a group of misfits—there are always a few misfits in the Army who don't seem to be able to tell their right leg from their left, and Bluey Britton was one of them—were getting sent back to Sydney Showgrounds for reassessment.

I organized myself to go with them. And we arrived back in the Showgrounds, spent a few weeks there and we were shipped up to Tamworth.

Tamworth was a training depot for the 2/18th, 2/19th, 2/20th Battalions. We didn't know who the devil they were but Blue and I were in the company that was 2/19th. That was the same as Mac Reid and Jimmy Arthur-Smith. Mac and I became good friends and we were both keen photographers and took a lot of photographs.

---

[8] The 2/33rd Battalion eventually became part of the 7th Division.

*Figure 2: Members of the 2/19ᵗʰ Battalion
detrain before shipping to Malaya. (AWM 005472)*

One day, a group of five men joined the unit, amongst them one Charlie Forrester. I gathered later that Charlie was a small-time bad lad from Sydney where he'd made his living as a petty thief and expert pickpocket. He was about nineteen, friendly, bright and cheerful and I was told that he had made so many appearances before the magistrate that he had been given the choice of going to jail or joining the army. Charlie couldn't drill, march, or anything else that a soldier was supposed to do, until came the day when all men were required to attend the rifle range and fire off ten rounds.

I was again made an instructor for the day and Charlie, of all people, appeared before me. I went through all the required instructions finishing with, "Then squeeze the trigger."

"Like this?" said Charlie and promptly scored a bullseye.

From ten shots, Charlie scored ninety from a possible one hundred.

He could shoot as well as me. I never could find out how a city-bred lad like him learned to use a rifle as well as he did.

Tamworth was an entirely different town to Dubbo. It was terribly conservative and closed up at nighttime. You could always get a drink though. Cafes were open and with the pub, you had to go in the back door. But nothing else happened. There were no attempts to entertain the troops, no dances, no nothing. Anyway, that didn't worry anyone and after about a month at Dubbo, we were all kitted up and had our dog tags stamped and our blood groups taken.

We were going off overseas. I'd had two lots of embarkation leave, one from Dubbo and another one from Tamworth and I was able to keep in touch with the family and Mavis[9] and let them know where I was going.

---

[9] Bill's girlfriend/fiancée, later wife, Mavis Walker.

# SHIPPING OFF TO WAR

———— ◆◇◆ ————

**W**e went by train down to Darling Harbour where we boarded an old passenger ship, probably 10,000 tons, called the 'Sibajak'[10]. She was an ex Dutch/East Indies ship.

All the crew were foreigners, Malays mostly, a few Chinese and the ship was of course crowded, but comfortable enough. We slept in hammocks; it was the first time I had ever slept in one. Very comfortable actually.

When we got just off Melbourne, turning into the (*Great Australian*) Bight, we picked up another ship. I think it was the 'Mauretania'[11] and an escort warship. Then across the Bight— well, I don't know how long it took us to cross. I think it might have been five or six days. They said afterward it was the roughest anybody had every known the Bight to be.

---

[10] Possibly the MS Sibajak, a Dutch passenger ship converted to a troop transport in about May of 1941.

[11] The RMS Mauretania, a British passenger ship converted to a troop transport.

AUSTRALIAN WAR MEMORIAL                                        007063

*Figure 3: Troop Transport Mauretania at anchor,*
*Sydney Harbour c. May 1941. (AWM 007063)*

That damn ship spent more time underwater than on top and everyone was seasick although Mac, Jimmy, and I found out that if we stayed upstairs on the deck and didn't eat anything except SAO biscuits (*a type of cracker biscuit*), we could handle the seasickness.

That was no problem.

We arrived in Perth and then found out that the glass windows on the bridge—which was sixty feet above water—had been broken by the waves. Not all of them, but most of them. We had to wait in port while that was repaired and it took about three days, I think. No leave, but that didn't stop us. Mac, Jimmy, and I crawled through a porthole and up on the wharf, and we wandered up into town.

We spent all day rambling around Perth, had a feed and a beer or two and one elderly gentleman walked up to us.

We were standing on a corner after just wandering around, and he said, "You boys look a bit lost. Would you like to go for a drive?"

Why not?

So damn it if he didn't go and get his motor car, petrol rationing and all, and he drove us for over an hour around Perth, up Queens Park, all over the place and we had a good look at the place—a beautiful city.

We took the same way back, got on board, and in due course, we sailed off.

Wasn't long after we left Perth that the cruiser that was escorting us, which was the 'HMAS Sydney', disappeared—shot off to the west.

She eventually met the German raider and never came back[12].

We had been at sea a couple of days and comforts were distributed. They had the usual razor blades and tobacco and a bit of chocolate and they also had some beautiful woollen socks, scarves, and balaclavas. We knew by then that we were going to Singapore, so we threw the balaclavas and scarves over the side.

---

[12] HMAS Sydney (D48) sank in a mutually destructive battle with the German cruiser SMS Kormoran (HSK-8) on the 19th November 1941.

# SINGAPORE

———— ◆◇◆ ————

Arrived in Singapore one morning (*February or March 1941*) and the first impression we got was of the heat. We had been hot before in western New South Wales and all over the place, but nothing like the heat and humidity of Singapore. It hits you. Anyway, off the ship, into trucks and onto the General Base Depot (*GBD*) in Johor Bahru, Malaysia which was across Singapore Island, across the causeway and about twelve miles into Johor Bahru on the mainland (*Malaysia*) was the General Base Depot which was the staging camp for all troops that came into Malaya.

An enormous camp—I don't know how many, but sixty or seventy acres covered with wood huts. Very well set up, of course, but there wasn't much put up for us, so we were in tents.

And for the first few days, we were getting acclimatized.

Jimmy and Mac were there. Bluey Britton was around somewhere, but I'd lost contact with Blue and I never saw him again until after we got home. Blue's problem was that he couldn't take the sun. He was red-haired, very fair complexion and if he got out, he got sunburnt, particularly in that hot Malay sun.

I think he must have finished up in an inside job somewhere.

Our first week there was spent acclimatizing in what they called the 'bull ring' (*Army slang for training ground*). The company I was in, there were about 100 of us on a stretch of ground, hot and dry, dusty—and we drilled. We drilled and drilled and drilled all day. The object of it was to sort out those who couldn't take it and they got hauled off home probably or something.

We all survived, but after being there a week, a Sergeant came around and selected a platoon of us. Not all 19th; there were 18th, 19th and 20th.

We were told to be ready to move out the next morning with all our gear. That was where I parted company with Mac and Jimmy. I didn't see Mac again and didn't meet up with Jimmy until after the surrender.

# ADVENTURES IN KUALA LUMPUR

——— ◆ ◇ ◆ ———

We were put on a train and went up to Kuala Lumpur (KL). There, we were taken to a village called Sentul which was about seven or eight miles north of KL; that was where Administrative Headquarters was situated in what had been a school, and we were the guard.

We had a guardhouse near the entrance and the usual attap hut[13] (*thatched roof house*) next door where we slept and charpoy beds to sleep on. A charpoy bed was a wooden framework with rattan fibre laced in between to make a flexible mattress. Very comfortable—you just put your blanket down on that. We all had mosquito nets. We didn't need anything on top of us, it was so damned hot. And they were very comfortable to sleep in.

---

[13] A type of thatched house, common in Singapore, Malaysia, and Indonesia. *Attap* literally translates as 'roof'.

AUSTRALIAN WAR MEMORIAL                                P01295.003

*Figure 4: Male staff HQ (attap huts)*
*at 2/10ᵗʰ Australian General Hospital. (AWM P01295.003)*

This was still peacetime in the Pacific of course, about October 1941 (*Japan entered the war on 7ᵗʰ December 1941*) and there was no war in Malaya then.

We had leave and went to KL once a week.

The school there—our headquarters—was surrounded by houses, mostly Chinese, some Indians and they never seemed to sleep. They had gramophones going night and day with their music playing and we wandered around all over the place when we weren't on duty. It was fascinating.

About a quarter of a mile away, there was a tin dredge operating; they made their own lake, and just kept on dredging the dirt up and making the lake bigger and bigger and bigger and using the water over and over again.

No shortage of water there; it rained nearly every day.

By now, we had got used to the heat and the humidity, but still found it a bit trying if we had to go around the streets for several miles. But it was a cushy job being the guard on the gates. Two men during the day, and at nighttime, we had a couple of roving pickets (*a group of soldiers on patrol, guard, or similar duty*) wandering around the buildings.

At the gate, we were supposed to search all the servants as they went out to make sure they weren't taking too many foodstuffs with them.

There was a number one boy, the head provedore who looked after the kitchen and supervising, and he was a very important person, the number one boy.

We always found something in their things, but we never took it off them.

Poor beggars, they weren't getting much tucker and weren't getting an awful lot of pay and we sort of closed the eyes to what they took.

Kuala Lumpur was terribly, terribly British, of course. You would walk into a photo shop to get some films processed or buy a film and there would be an English woman standing next to you and you'd look around and smile, and she would look the other way.

She wasn't going to speak to some common Private soldier.

But they were all right; it was just the way they were brought up and we met a few of the men around the place occasionally, and they were very decent types.

Johnny Bell and I had become good friends and we used to, any time we had off, hire bicycles and ride all over the town—a very beautiful town, Kuala Lumpur. I remember one time we went to the pictures and as usual, we found it very cheap. I can't remember what it was, but everything was much cheaper than it was at home. We bought seats in the dress circle.

We were late. We squeezed in amongst a lot of other bods and anyhow, it came to the interval—I don't remember what picture was on—and the lights came on and we were surrounded by all the top brass of the British Army. Here were Colonels, and Generals and Red Caps *(UK Royal Military Police)* everywhere.

We were the only Private soldiers in the place upstairs and knowing us, of course, we went down to the lobby and bought ourselves a beer and were standing around having a smoke. And an Englishman in civvies came up and said hello and we got talking, saying who we were and whatever. And he said, "I'll tell you what, after the show, come back to my place for a snifter."

Good, so we met him downstairs after the show.

His car drove up with a chauffeur, a syce (*an attendant*) they called them. He drove up and we hopped in and went around to his home—beautiful home. His wife was away, he was lonely and wanted someone to talk to and we spent an hour or two there, had a few whiskeys and whatever and the driver came around and drove us back to camp.

There were two dance halls in Kuala Lumpur where anybody could go in, and you bought a ticket and that gave you the right to have a dance with one of the hostesses. It was strictly dancing only, nothing else and they were good places to go. The beer was cheap. Tiger beer is very good and always icy cold. We used to go in there occasionally, and every now and then, it was our team's turn to mount the picket on the dance halls. We were supposed to go in fully armed, tin hats and all on, and we were supposed to go in and keep the peace.

If anybody played up rough, we were supposed to stop them.

We couldn't give a damn about that.

We would go into the dance hall, pick a table right in the corner somewhere, put our tin hats on the floor underneath, and take our MP armbands off.

Then, the proprietor would give us free beer all night.

We were in one of the dance halls one night and after a few beers, there were a few pommy (*British*) soldiers and one of the guys was at a table near us and the British MPs came in, the Red Caps. They were hated people too, as they were vicious. And this poor beggar had the collar of his jacket undone. The MP's lumbered him—*you are incorrectly dressed and you're under arrest*—so the Red Caps dragged him out where the paddy wagon was waiting.

There were about half a dozen of us there and some more Australians somewhere across the hall, and we sort of wandered out.

This seemed a bit rough to us and a few words were said, and the MP's didn't like us and we didn't like them—and all of a sudden, the back of the paddy wagon was open and the pommy sergeant was gone. He'd scarpered. Well, that got the Red Caps mad and they were going to arrest us. We stood off and abused them and they abused us and in a very short time, there were about fifty Australians on one side of the street and about fifty Red Caps on the other and an officer in the middle trying to keep us apart. War damn nearly broke out there and then, but common sense prevailed. The Red Caps went home, and we went home, but the rule after that was that we were to leave the Red Caps alone and they would not touch us under any circumstances.

# THE TRANSPORT UNIT

———— ◆ ◇ ◆ ————

Towards the end of October, Admin Headquarters was packing up and going back to Johor Bahru, and the officers said, "Can any of you blokes drive?"

I said, "Yes sir, I can drive a car and a motorcycle, and I can drive a truck."

Johnny Bell said the same thing. He had never driven a truck in his life, and I had only driven one once. Anyway, lo and behold, a truck appeared, and we were given a driving test and we both passed—just. When we got back to Johor Bahru, we went back to the same GBD *(General Base Depot)* as before but on the outskirts of it. Admin set up their headquarters there, and now they had a transport group attached to them. Divisional Headquarters was the brains trust of the division.

Divisional Headquarters made the decisions and Admin Headquarters carried them out. Troops moved here, troops moved there, troops wanted supplies and ammunition, and Admin Headquarters organised it.

AUSTRALIAN WAR MEMORIAL                                        008502

*Figure 5: New trucks from Australia arrive in Singapore*
*c. July 1941. (AWM 008502)*

The head man of Admin Headquarters was Lieutenant Colonel Kent Hughes.

He was a thorough gentleman and he made it after the war into Parliament, and I think he became Sir Wilfred Kent Hughes[14].

But we established a transport unit. We had two trucks—two Chevy maple-leaf trucks, a couple of utilities, about four cars and a motorcycle despatch rider. I was quite a capable car driver and it didn't take me long to learn to drive the Chevy truck. The ones we had were

---

[14] Sir Wilfred Kent Hughes, KBE, MVO, MC was an Australian politician. Notably, he served in World War II without resigning from Parliament.

the same as the ones sent to the Middle East, with the big track grip tyres on them.

No synchromesh on the gear box, of course, but an easy truck to drive.

We were all indoctrinated into the procedures for starting up and getting ready to drive and driving in convoy and that sort of thing. It was still a fairly easy task there. We were in tents. The rest of the mob, in Admin Headquarters, were in wooden huts. The transport mob, about a dozen of us, were in tents, again with charpoys and nets and we had our own ablution block nearby, but still it was peacetime, and we never did our own laundry work.

The dhobi walla (*literally, washer man*), a local, came around every day and got our shirts and shorts and the next day they came back beautifully washed and ironed at 5c. per article. You wouldn't waste your own time washing your own clothes for 5c.

They were Malay cents.

I think there were about four Malay dollars to the Australian pound.

Our transport group was designed to take quick action somewhere if something was wanted in a hurry. Rather than pass the word back through the ASC[15] (*Army Service Corp*) channels or somewhere, rather than wait, we were sent out to do the job. We carried ammunition and supplies and men here and there, and we went out into the scrub with half a dozen Tamils and filled the truck up with wood to keep the cookhouse fires going.

---

[15] ASC, Army Service Corp. Responsible for administration, supply, and logistics e.g. food, water, fuel, etc.

# PRELUDE TO CONFLICT

———————————— ◆ ◇ ◆ ————————————

W e had a lot of trips to Singapore. We were about five miles from GBD by the Johor Bahru-Singapore Island Causeway; there, you could pick up Woodland Road, which was a beautiful road, a real racetrack. Into Bukit Timah Circuit and into the main Singapore city.

If we happened to be in Singapore at lunchtime or thereabouts, we called into the British Services Club which had been established on Padang right in the middle of Singapore.

The British wives did a hell of a good job there; they were civilian wives. They provided a meal of bangers and mash and a cup of coffee and you paid about 10c or something.

But things were pretty easy at that stage.

About two weeks before the day the war started, we were all told something was cooking and we had to be prepared for active service. That meant that the trucks which were a light fawn colour had to be camouflaged. Well, that was quite simple; we got tins of paint and we splashed paint all over the trucks. The ignition keys were welded into the locks so they couldn't be lost. We were all issued with twenty rounds of live ammunition. The only problem was that in the truck, there was nowhere to put your rifle. We were supposed to have clamps on the dashboard so you could clamp your rifle upright there, but we didn't have them.

We were also supposed to have pistols, but there weren't enough to go around and the officers grabbed all the pistols and we had none. But I had taken over with me my father's Colt 32-calibre automatic. I got it working and I had one of the locals make me a holster for it, and I put up the holster on the steering column and kept my pistol there.

AUSTRALIAN WAR MEMORIAL                    116470

*Figure 6: 2/13th Australian General Hospital (AGH)*
*c. 1945. (AWM 116470)*

We were all drilled about air raids and all had dispersal points. There was a bit of a hill where we were, not a big hill, a few hundred feet above the rest and on top of it was the 2/13th Australian General Hospital (AGH)[16]. My dispersal point was not far from the AGH, up that hill.

---

[16] As of 2020, operating as St Patrick's Boys School, Singapore.

# JAPAN ENTERS THE FRAY

———— ◆ ◇ ◆ ————

A woke on December 7ᵗʰ 1941 to the air raid alarm going off. While we'd had a few trials before this, someone shouted this was for real, so we all turned out.

We all slept fully clothed. Once you had your shower at night, you were fully clad in uniforms, boots and all and we were out into the truck, drove it up to the dispersal point and I could see Singapore from there, way in the distance.

Singapore was a blaze of lights; anti-aircraft shells were flying all over the place and I mean *really* all over the place, shooting at nothing at all.

I saw one plane, I think it was probably the last plane to go over and drop his bombs and once he disappeared, Singapore's lights all went out. A bit late.

*Figure 7: Singapore Air Raid Precautions (ARP) volunteer workers fighting fires caused by Japanese Bombs January 2nd 1942. (AWM 012450)*

The next day, I was in Singapore on a job and went down to where the raid had taken place, mainly in the Chinese section, down towards the docks.

They'd dropped five bombs; there were five planes, I believe, carrying one apiece. They didn't do an awful lot of damage but that was where it all started.

The first thing that happened after the show commenced was the fifth column (*enemy sympathizers*) started to operate. They were mostly Indian. The Indians didn't like the British and some of them seemed to be quite happy to hand over the whole country to the Japs. Every now and then, one of the fifth column would take a pot shot at you as you drove past. You didn't know where the hell he was; you couldn't see him but there would be the odd shot whistle overhead or slam into the mudguard somewhere.

They never did much damage; I think they were only very light rifles.

Another one of the fifth-column tricks was to stretch a wire across the road between a couple of rubber trees and they were aiming particularly for motorcycles, despatch riders or if the wire was heavy enough, they could cause a bit of damage to a car but they wouldn't worry a truck much.

There was always a bit of humour, even in the shooting war.

Johnny Bell was a car driver and one day, they must have been short of drivers, I drew the short straw.

The Sergeants called out, "Lofty[17], you have to take Captain Shearing into Singapore."

Well, I knew Captain Shearing.

Charlie Shearing—before the war—had been a cab driver in Sydney. Sydney cab drivers were a race apart. Charlie was no exception. He wasn't very tall. He was talkative, aggressive and he was rude. He was arrogant and in other words, was a real dickhead. But we never took much notice of him and the cars we were driving were Chevys and they were real bombs.

So, Charlie climbed in the back seat and we were off to Singapore.

After we got across the Causeway and onto Woodland Road, Charlie said, "Can't we go any faster, driver? I'm in a hurry." I had the thing flat to the boards then and we were doing about seventy mph. "Sorry, Sir, this is as fast as she will go."

---

[17] Bill Lowcock was 6'2" and known to his comrades as Lofty.

We got down to the dock area at Keppel Harbour and went to the big sheds, enormous great things, and Charlie said, "Stop here." So, I came to a gentle stop about fifteen or twenty yards down and Charlie went off like a bundle of crackers (*fireworks*).

"I didn't say to stop *here,* driver. I said to stop *there.*"

"Yes, Sir."

I put the car in reverse, and we backed up and Charlie got out.

And he got back in later.

"Alright, driver," he said, "Straight ahead."

So I picked up a bit of speed and was doing about twenty-five mph, and it was a beautiful bitumen surface and a long way to go. And I knew what was going to happen.

Charlie said, "Alright driver, stop here."

Well, the Chevys might not have gone very hard, but they sure stopped quick. I reckon I buried the nose of that car in the dirt. I was sitting there looking straight ahead with my hands on the wheel—no seat belts in those days and all bench seats.

Lo and behold, there was Charlie folded neatly over the back of the passenger seat next to me. He unwound himself and I picked his hat up off the floor and gave it back to him. I'll say this for the beggar – he never said a bloody word. He went about his business and came back in the car and we drove back to base. I never drove Charlie after that.

It was about this time that the 'Prince of Wales' and the 'Repulse'[18] sank and that was a real catastrophe *(10th December 1941)*.

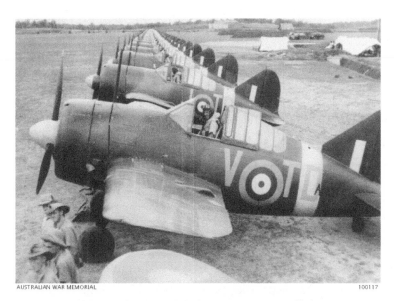

AUSTRALIAN WAR MEMORIAL                                                    100117

*Figure 8: RAAF RAF Brewster Buffalo*
*aircraft of 453 Squadron on Sembawang Airfield.*
*c. 1941 (AWM 100117)*

I was in at the ASC (*Army Service Corps*) depot in Johor Bahru one morning when the Jap carrier planes came over. Our fellows from Seletar Base on the island took off to have a go at them. The Japanese Zero then was a very upmarket aircraft. They were very manoeuvrable, quite fast and our poor beggars, all they had was the Brewster Buffalo, an American machine which was obsolete about five or six years before. It was a damn shame to watch. They shot our fellows out of the air one by one.

---

[18] HMS Prince of Wales and HMS Repulse were sunk by bombers of the Imperial Japanese Navy. Survivors were taken to Singapore.

# MOTORCYCLE DESPATCH

Our despatch rider was a young Greek, Nick. I don't know what his second name was since I could hardly pronounce it, so he became Nick the Greek. Nick was a fairly cheerful young bloke and he was out riding one day. The roads then were beautiful roads, all bitumen with big ditches on either side to carry the rain off. You never got stopped by the rain on the road in Malaya.

Nick was off on his bike one day and he ran into a wire strapped across the road. The fifth columns used to stretch piano wire if they could get it, between a couple of rubber trees.

The idea was to catch the rider, not the bike. Because if you are doing fifty mph down the road and you run into a piece of piano wire, then that's the finish of you.

Nick was lucky as the wire caught onto the handlebars of the bike and it tipped him and the bike into the ditch. He broke an arm and a leg and got sent home. He was lucky.

I was the only other member of our team who was licensed to ride a motorcycle. So, the Sergeant called me over and said, "Alright, Lofty, you're the despatch rider until we can get a replacement."

I said, "Righto Sarge, but what do I drive? Nick's machine's a write-off."

He said, "We won't have another machine here for a day or two, see what you can do."

In those days in the Army, it was called scrounging.

In civilian life, it was called theft.

It was very definite rules in the Army. You never scrounged from your own team or mob or platoon, but you scrounged from the platoon or the company next door. But you only scrounged Army paraphernalia, nothing personal was ever taken—as that would be theft.

What I wanted was a motorcycle, and GBD was a staging camp for all troops that came into that country; there were troops flying through the place all the time. A lot of British and quite a few Australians were coming in. I decided to take a walk down to where there were a couple of huts down from where we were camped. Lo and behold, I walked in between these two huts and there was a motorcycle sitting up on its stand, right there.

In those days, all the cycles were British, apart from the American Harley Davidson, as Mr. Honda hadn't made his mark at that time. The pick of the bikes was the Norton,[19] and the Matchless[20] was not far behind and this machine I was looking at was a Matchless.

I sauntered around a bit. I wasn't going to show any interest in it. I walked around the back of the huts and the huts were all empty and went around the back of the cookhouse and the cookhouse was empty too. The whole place was empty, so I went back and had another look at this machine. It had fifteen miles on the odometer. It was a 350cc brand-new overhead-valve, four-speed foot change. The key was in

---

[19] Norton Motorcycle Company, a British motorcycle manufacturer.
[20] Matchless, a British motorcycle company.

the ignition of it and the owner was nowhere in sight. I very smartly pulled it off its stand and wheeled it very quickly back to our own lines.

We checked the petrol tank and the oil tank, and they were both full. Turned it on, the battery was right, but it wouldn't start. Anyway, we didn't take long to figure that out. We pulled the cap off the magneto points and the guy who had owned it evidently knew a bit about it, and he had a piece of cigarette paper in between the points. This meant it would never start like that so we took that out and away she went. I spent about a week on that machine, despatch riding all over Singapore and wherever, and I'd never had any chance of ever owning a bike this good. It was a real beauty. I think I clocked about ninety mph down Woodland Road one day.

Then we got a new DonR[21] (*Despatch Rider*) and I went back to driving the truck.

---

[21] The Don in DonR comes from the WW2 UK phonetic alphabet, Ack, Beer, Cork, Don, Eddy, Freddy, George, etc. Don for Despatch and R for Rider.

# BOMBING RAIDS

———— ◆ ◇ ◆ ————

We were supposed to carry observers on our trucks. That was to act as a lookout for air raids or strafing, but we never had enough men, so we always drove alone. We were getting quite busy now, driving all over the place. I was told one day to pick up a load of hospital supplies and equipment and take it up to Malacca which was on the west coast.

Malacca is a very old Portuguese town, much older than Singapore itself. We were supposed to drive at nighttime because there were a few Jap strafing planes making their presence felt around the place, so I took off just before dark one afternoon.

Just as I was leaving, the Sergeant said, "You had better watch yourself on this one, Lofty, there are stories about Jap infiltrators somewhere in that area."

He was a real comforting bloke, this Sergeant.

Anyway, I had been going for about an hour or an hour and a half.

In daylight, the trip would take about three hours. But at nighttime, with no moon, blacked-out lights, the maximum speed you could get up to was probably twenty-five to thirty mph, so I was looking at a six or seven-hour drive.

I had been going for about an hour and could just vaguely see a hut on the side of the road, and across the road was a blooming great barrier covered with barbed wire. It blocked the road completely. Nobody had told me anything about this, so I sort of played it by keeping the motor running. Then I saw a short figure with what appeared to be a big long rifle on his shoulder, coming towards me from the hut. I got my pistol out, safety catch off. I figured if this was a Jap, I'd take him out and then I'd push the end of that barrier out and be long gone before his mates knew what'd happened. I had the truck in gear and the trucks were quite high off the ground and to get into the cabin, you had to climb onto the running board.

Anyway, this bloke did exactly that and as he stuck his head into the window, I stuck the sharp end of the pistol onto his chin and I was getting ready to pull the bloody trigger.

He yelled one word which proved that he wasn't a Japanese and he wasn't British, and he wasn't Indian. He said, "Shit," which meant he had to be Australian, and then he shone his torch on himself and damn it if it wasn't a bloke I had come over on the ship with. After he said a few more well-chosen words, he said *you had better come in, we've got the billy*[22] *boiling, have a cuppa and some food.* I went around to the back of the hut and found a four-gallon tin of tea boiling up and we had a feed of a bit of bully beef (*tinned corned beef*) and some biscuits.

They didn't know what or why they were there.

They were simply supposed to check whatever was coming along the road, but they knew as much about it as I did. But anyway, I went on to Malacca and unloaded my truck, and I always carried a charpoy in the back. I pulled the charpoy down and slept until dawn. Then I went around to the cookhouse and scrounged a feed and drove back home.

---

[22] A "Billy" is a lightweight can or pot used for cooking. Immortalized in the Australian Song "Waltzing Matilda".

By this time, the Japanese were stepping up their bombing raids on Singapore. They used to send over about thirty or forty planes at a time, always in V formation, and we believe that the leading plane had the bomb sites and they all dropped their bombs in one heap whenever they came. They were very methodical people, the Japanese.

They came over twice a day – usually about nine or ten o'clock in the morning and four o'clock in the afternoon, so the general idea was that you tried not to be in Singapore at those times.

They also bombed the town of Johor Bahru very heavily. There were large railway marshalling yards there and they knocked them about considerably.

About the middle of January, I had to escort and take a load of Malay Police to Jemaluang on the east coast of the mainland, about four- or five-hours' drive from Johor Bahru.

I had a truck load of equipment and half a dozen constables in the back of my truck and a Corporal in the cabin with me, and behind was the boss man. I don't know what rank or who he was. He was a Malay, driving with a driver in a Vauxhall car.

We arrived at Jemaluang late in the afternoon. It was just in from the coast on the banks of a river. There was a clearing in the jungle where someone had been camped.

I found out later it was the 2/19th Battalion.

The only people in evidence there at that time were a group of Signals (*military communication*).

There was one group on the other side of the river and three or four of them on this side.

We had a bit of a yarn and I decided I would spend the night there.

I had some food with me and would drive back the next day.

I was just getting ready to make arrangements, when out of the jungle came a Lieutenant, a Sergeant and half a dozen men carrying a lot of gear with them. They turned out to be from the 2/19th. They had been up the river on reconnaissance and the battalion had moved out while they were away and gone up to Muar.

*Figure 9: Members of I Section Reconnaissance,*
*2/19th Battalion AIF. (AWM P00102.042)*

I have never been able to find out the name of the Lieutenant, but I think he might have been Lieutenant (*John Ashton*) Varley. Anyway, he asked me what I was doing there, and I told him, and he said, "Alright, you're commandeered." Well, that suited me, I wasn't going anywhere else.

We loaded them all on the truck and we set out. We didn't go back on the road we had come by. This fellow knew where he was going and we went across the country through a lot of jungle tracks and drove until ten or eleven o'clock at night and came out at Kluang.

I had been to Kluang several times before; it was about a hundred miles north of Johor and they had an aerodrome nearby that the RAF had established, and a small village was not far from the RAF base.

The whole place was a mass of vehicles going here, there and everywhere, a blaze of lights. It appeared the RAF station was being evacuated down south.

Of course, with them going and the Japs not all that far away, the village was going too and the poor old locals were loading everything they could onto some cars and carts and moving off down south. In the middle of the village square was a very large Australian MP Sergeant, directing traffic and trying to solve a bit of confusion. I pulled up next to him.

He said, "Where the hell do you think you're going?"

Then we looked at each other and I realized it was Gordon Schultz. He'd been a Private in the guard that we'd had at Kuala Lumpur in the previous October. A nice cove too.

I said to Gordon, "Look, the blokes in the back are short of smokes. Is there anything we can do about that?" He said, "Wait here." And he walked away and about five minutes later, he came back with three cartons of Players which were tossed into the back.

A very popular man was Gordon at that moment.

We pulled out of town a little way. I and all the boys were bushed, so we parked the truck on the side of the road, and all went to sleep, right where we sat.

I woke up at dawn, had a bit of bully beef and biscuits and moved on.

Eventually, we came to a place not far from Yong Peng. Pulled up off the road into another jungle clearing and there were trucks and men and everybody everywhere and this was the 2/19th Battalion assembly point before they moved up to Muar.

I got out of the truck and looked around, and a young chap came walking down the road towards me and we looked at each other—and it was Peter Howse.

Peter Howse came from Orange where I had lived when I was a small boy.

When I was about six years old, I'd spent some time at school with Peter.

When I found out where we were, I asked the Officer if I could stay with the battalion.

After all, I came with reinforcements for them.

Despite my pleading with them, the answer was no, and I went back to base at Johor Bahru.

I was driving one time out on a very narrow road through the jungle towards the Seletar Air Base. I noticed on the side of the road hidden amongst the long grass, these enormous great wooden packing cases. Some of them were thirty to forty feet long and they had to be airplanes in a knockdown state, and I found out later that they were Hurricanes.

AUSTRALIAN WAR MEMORIAL                                        SUK15202

*Figure 10: Hawker Hurricane fighter aircraft*
*(V7476) evacuated from Singapore c. 1942. (AWM SUK15202)*

They were sent out from Britain, hopefully to be reassembled and put into the air. In Singapore shortly afterwards, I was there when an air raid came over. Thirty planes or so, they were very high up at about 20,000 feet, flying in a beautiful V formation. Although the Brits had brought some 4" ack-ack guns from the UK, they weren't very effective against planes at that height.

Then I saw three Hurricanes. They must have been 10,000 feet up and then all of a sudden, they went straight up vertically, then very neatly picked off the first three Jap planes which disintegrated—and the rest of them, of course, dispersed and went for their lives.

Unfortunately, the Japs from then on concentrated their efforts on the airfield at Seletar and made it uninhabitable, and we understand the Hurricanes were later flown out to Java.

# THE BATTLE OF SINGAPORE

——— ◆ ◇ ◆ ———

Towards the end of January, the big evacuation from the mainland took place and we were going all day and all night, and when we got back to our base, we found it was evacuated anyway.

The base was moved back to Holland Road on Singapore Island and by now, the Japs had occupied the Kluang Airfield (*27th January 1942*) with their Zeros, which brought them within an easy distance of Singapore Island itself. Strafing became very frequent.

Almost every day, you went out and some Kamikaze Jap pilot would want to add your truck to his record, and I had some pretty narrow escapes. I lost one truck on the road.

I wasn't in it, of course, as I had devised a very quick way of getting out of the machine. You could see the plane coming at you from half a mile away. They always attacked from the front. If they had come at you from the back, they would have had a lot more success because you could see them coming from the front.

Getting out of the truck was the hardest part because you had to turn off the ignition, pull on the handbrake and then open the door, reaching out behind you. I devised a system where I had the door open but held in place with a very strong piece of string around the door handle clasp and inside the truck. All I had to do was switch off the ignition, pull the handbrake on and push the door open, and I could be in the gutter in five seconds flat.

About the last week in January, the mainland was finally evacuated, and the Causeway was blown up (*31st January 1942*) and everybody was back on the island. We were at Holland Road I think, for about four or five days and late one afternoon, the word came: evacuate, get out quick.

*Figure 11: Singapore Causeway with seventy-foot*
*gap blown by withdrawing forces,*
*31st January 1942. (AWM 012467)*

We moved all our trucks up to the main store place where all the records were kept and they said, "You've got ten minutes to be out." We loaded the trucks up like crazy and loaded all the guys on board and scarpered back towards the city.

I found out later that five minutes after we had left, the Japs had come over and flattened the place.

We moved into a place called Holland House, a big old building, just on the top of the hill not far from Bukit Timah Circuit.

We moved in there, I suppose about four o'clock in the afternoon.

I was sent out on a job somewhere, driving one of the utilities.

All our trucks were parked around the place, and blokes dug trenches, and no one knew what the hell was going to happen next. I was away for about an hour and I came back and found that the Japs had again bombed the joint.

For some reason, they perhaps thought that we were Divisional Headquarters.

Of course, they knew exactly where everybody was because the fifth columnists had a system going where they would tell them exactly where every unit was.

They knocked out all our trucks and this was where poor old Peter Pollard[23] got killed.

Poppa Pollard, we called him. He drove the other truck the same as mine, and we called him Poppa because his son was born after he arrived in Malaya.

We buried Peter there, and then we were told to move out on foot as the only vehicle operating was the ute I had. Somebody took that and the rest of us moved out on foot, back down to Bukit

---

[23] There is no record in the AWM online archives of Peter Pollard. There is a Laurence Eli Pollock NX26364 2/19th d.19.01.1942 and an Oswald James Pollett NX29686 attached to the AIF HQ d.11.02.1942. Either of whom may have been known as Peter, but this is not confirmed.

Timah Circuit and then back into Singapore city, where we were bunked in what had been an army storehouse.

There was a lot of confusion in the city at that time.

The Japs had landed, pushed our fellows back and had broken through at Kranji Airport (*7th February 1942*). We spent the night in the storehouse.

The next morning, I got up at dawn, looking for something to eat and somebody produced some bread rolls. Where they got them from, I've got no idea. I scrounged around and found a tin of butter and got that open with my bayonet. I had a bread roll in one hand and was scooping the butter out of the tin with the other, and a shell dropped right outside the window on the road. Blew the window all over me and covered this bread roll and the tin of butter with powdered glass. It was damned annoying because I was looking forward to that food.

Another five shells dropped there in the next few minutes, and we were lucky, because if they had moved their sights a fraction, they'd have dropped right on top of our building.

In hindsight, I knew why we were shelled.

The previous night, I had seen a torch flashing from the top of a building across the street. It had a flat roof with a steel walkway up the side. The sergeant and I went to investigate and found one of the fifth column, with a torch. I was all for shooting him, but the Sergeant decided he should be handed over to the police.

We were told to get ready to move out. We were going back to Tanglin Barracks near the Botanical Gardens. A couple of us went out to see what we could do. Outside the building were five Ford trucks that had been parked overnight. When we examined them, most had flat tyres where the shells had punched holes in them.

Anyway, with quite a bit of effort, out of the four trucks we found, we finished up with one with four good tyres on it. I got in to check it over, put my foot on the foot brake and it went right to the floor; it had no brakes. I went back to the other trucks and they were all the same.

I never found out whether it was the shockwave from the shells that blew them out or whether someone had sabotaged them. We put the first load of men and equipment on and to get to Tanglin Barracks, we had to go down Orchard Road which at that time had a large park on one side and houses on the other side. It ran very straight for perhaps a mile straight through the centre of the city, straight out to the Botanical Gardens.

The only problem was that on the first trip out, we found that the Japs had the road under observation and were lobbing mortar bombs all the way around. It was quite an exciting ride. I was doing about 60 mph down this road with mortar shells lobbing all over the place and guys in the back cheering their heads off.

When I got to the end of the road, of course, I had no brakes.

All I could do was pull the handbrake on and pick up a lower gear. I made, I think, six trips that day. We had an awful lot of near misses, but we were lucky.

We pulled into Tanglin, on top of the hill. It had been a British Army Camp. Very nicely done out, with beautiful huts everywhere and the guard room at the entrance to the barracks was where the Divisional Headquarters were.

The frontline, we thought, was perhaps half a mile away. From then on, we became largely infantry because there was very little petrol around. The Japs captured the base ordinance depot where the ammunition was and captured the oil supply depot.

There just wasn't anything to take anywhere so we disabled the truck and then we dug slit trenches. We became infantry, and our job from then on was said to be guarding Divisional Headquarters. We mounted a guard around it, a patrolling picket.

That last week—one unusual job I had—the Sergeant came around one night and said, "Lofty, I've got a job for you." We walked down the hill and outside the barracks, and somebody had scrounged a truck and we got in it and we drove down to the heart of the business area.

We backed the truck up to the side entrance to one of the banks, can't remember which one, and there were MPs everywhere.

The bank employees loaded the truck up with cash and notes all in bags.

God knows how many millions of dollars there were, and we drove down to the waterfront at Keppel Harbour, backed the truck up to the edge of the water and they threw the lot into the sea. I don't know whether any of the locals ever found it later, but there was an awful lot of coin there that somebody could have got.

The thing that I was annoyed about was that I could have reached over the back of my seat in the truck and grabbed a bag full of notes and nobody would have known the difference.

But I didn't bother.

By this time, the Japs had their mortars and artillery within easy range of the city and they for the last week, it was just a continual daylight bombardment.

They dropped mortars all over the city, all over us. We got a few casualties. During the daytime, there was nothing you could do.

If you moved outside, you were knocked over with mortar fire. We spent most of the daytime sitting at the bottom of a slit trench, waiting for something to happen. I remember I found a book in one of the huts nearby and spent my time reading it. There was nothing else to do.

At nighttime, we went out on patrols around Divisional Headquarters but didn't see anything extraordinary. But that last week was just one continuous barrage of shells and mortars. The Japs had a little Auster-type (*light observation plane*) aircraft that flew around the place at about forty mph and about 500 feet up almost, spotting. They knew exactly where everyone was. We had an ack-ack mount for a light automatic, and we had a Lewis gun and I pleaded with the Sergeant and another Officer, "Let me shoot that damn plane down." I could have done too, because I was a pretty good shot with a light automatic. "Oh no", he said, "You can't do that, you'll give our position away." I mean, what rot; the Japs knew exactly where we were anyway.

It has been said that the giant 16" guns mounted out near Changi, pointing to the sea, were never used. Well one of them was. Several times at night, one of these would be let off.

A most extraordinary sound, you would hear the boom when the thing was going off and then the shell going overhead sounded like a modern jet fighter—although we didn't have jet fighters in those days. And then about ten seconds later, the ground would shake.

These guns were probably ten miles away but one of them going would cause the ground under your feet to move quite appreciably. I think they fired probably half a dozen shots.

They must have got the thing traversed around sufficiently to get their bearings somewhere on Johor Bahru.

AUSTRALIAN WAR MEMORIAL                                                                 011597

*Figure 12: Gunners "Pulling Through" the barrel*
*of the Singapore gun after firing. (AWM 011597)*

# THE SURRENDER OF SINGAPORE

—————— ◆ ◇ ◆ ——————

Rumours started to circulate that there was to be a surrender, and nobody was very happy about that. It came on the 15th of February 1942 and at five o'clock in the afternoon, suddenly everything stopped. It was the most extraordinary feeling to have no noise.

For about eight days, we'd had nothing but a continuous bombardment of shells and mortars and now, complete silence. It had to come, of course.

With no air cover, no navy, and Jap fighting troops that had been based in China for years, highly experienced, highly trained and very efficient, we had little chance.

AUSTRALIAN WAR MEMORIAL                                    127902

*Figure 13: British Troops*
*Surrender to the Japanese (AWM 127902)*

The final reason for the surrender was that we ran out of water. Singapore's water then came along a pipeline from the mainland to a reservoir somewhere out near Changi.

But of course, once the Japs got to Johor Bahru and captured the area, they turned the water off. The reservoir ran dry and there were fires all over Singapore. The city itself was a shambles. There were a million civilian residents still there, and without water in that climate, you can't go for very long.

We were lucky where we were because the battalion barracks had a beautiful fifty-metre swimming pool attached to it and it was full of water, and so we had plenty.

No worries there and of course, when the show was over, all the locals came out and filled their water bottles and that was right.

Nothing happened the following day. We never saw any Japs, but we spent one more night there and then we were told that we were moving out. So, we marched from there out to the barracks at Changi, about fifteen miles. We carried what we had with us, which wasn't very much.

I had lost most of my personal gear when the truck was blown up. I had a pack and a water bottle. We, of course, had to hand our rifles in. I had our slouch hat, shirt, shorts, boots and a pair of socks and one or two items I had been able to keep.

The march out to Changi was a long hard one and what made it worse was the Japanese had compelled all the locals to line the side of the road all through the main city and we had a column of Australian, British and other troops marching through and it was most mortifying, to say the least. We felt considerably ashamed and let down.

Our group moved into the Selarang Barracks area which had previously been occupied by the Gordon Highlanders, a splendid square of three main three-storey buildings all done out in concrete, on a square—which was perhaps 100 yards square—in the middle. There were cookhouses behind and a few hundred yards away, the officers' mess and then the other houses for the non-commissioned officers and whatever. Then at the back of the whole complex was the well-equipped hospital.

AUSTRALIAN WAR MEMORIAL                                                                    132933

*Figure 14: Selarang Barracks POW Camp, Singapore*
*c. 1942 (AWM 132933)*

The whole area at Changi would probably cover fifty acres, all beautifully landscaped in impeccable condition.

Our biggest problem in the early days there was the food and boredom. People who had been used to living on meat etc. went back to living on rice with not much with it. There was plenty of water, thank goodness, as the water was turned back on but there was no electricity.

All the power stations were out of action. Our fellows couldn't use the modern kitchen attached to the base and so we had to use firewood everywhere.

We were kept busy digging latrines, cleaning up, getting the base in ship shape order and working parties into the bush to gather firewood, etc.

It was here that I caught up with Jimmy Arthur-Smith. He and the two Males boys (*Len and Dick)* were camped on the top floor of one of the buildings, not the same one that I was in.

When the Gordons occupied the building, they had steel beds to sleep in. Of course, they had all gone and we slept on the concrete floor. It was no problem. A blanket under, kit bag for a pillow, and the only problem was the bed bugs. The place was crawling with them.

With no DDT (*insecticide)* or anything else to combat the things, they made life a bit miserable for a while.

Up until now, I hadn't seen a Japanese.

There were no guards inside the camp, but we occasionally struck one or two of them when we were outside on working parties. These were Japanese frontline troops.

They caused us no problems and we had strict instructions to do what we were told.

One lasting memory I have of the early days in Changi was the fact that the British officers had the Officers' Mess going again, a large building set out on its own in the middle of beautiful lawns surrounded by coconut palms. At nighttime, Jimmy Arthur-Smith, the Males boys, and used to walk over close to this and somebody would be playing the piano, beautiful piano playing. And then at ten o'clock, the bugle would sound lights out and the piper would play the Highland Cradle Song. Whenever I hear that tune now, it brings back memories of those very early days, when we did not know what was going to happen in the day or month or week. We were just waiting to see what would transpire.

# A PRISONER OF WAR

———— ◆ ◇ ◆ ————

In about April or May 1942, a couple of hundred of us were marched into Singapore where we took up residence at the Great World[24]. This had been a dance hall and it was quite a large set of buildings, well weatherproofed, with wooden floors.

From there, we were sent on working parties into the docks in Singapore. Unloading ships, loading ships, carrying bags of rice and tins of food, and there was no shortage of food in the Great World because we used to bring home—against orders, of course—as much as we could smuggle out without getting caught. A tin of condensed milk would fit, uncomfortably, in the crotch of your shorts and your water bottle could be filled up with sugar and nobody would know the difference. If you were caught, of course, you got a bashing. But that was a fair risk.

The guards there were still Japanese soldiers. They didn't cause us any great deal of problems. We did what we were told. Got the occasional rifle butt in the back if you didn't move quickly enough but things weren't all too bad at the Great World. We ate well, and things were going quite well for me then until I caught dengue fever[25] and got sent back to Changi.

Dengue was just like a very bad attack of flu, but it lasted for a couple to three weeks and I got over it and rejoined the rest of the unit

---

[24] Great World: a former amusement park used by the Japanese as a POW camp.
[25] Dengue fever is a tropical disease, caused by the dengue virus and spread by mosquitos.

in Changi Barracks. Shortly after I recovered, a team of us was sent to Lornie Road on the outskirts of Singapore, right opposite the Singapore golf links. We were housed in about four very nice homes which had been presumably been occupied by the British people but there was no working sewerage, of course. We had to dig holes all over the lawns but there was a little bit of electricity, though of course, not very much.

And here we were engaged in building the shrine on top of the hill in the middle of the golf course. We also built bridges. The Japs brought Chinese stonemasons in to cut the most beautiful effigies to put on each end of the bridge. The workmanship was absolutely first class.

I think after the war it was all demolished, naturally.

But my job there was to row a barge. You probably have seen them row these great big barges with the oar at the back and you move it backwards and sideways, and after a little while, it becomes quite easy. I took the barge up a canal or lake in the middle of the golf course, then someone loaded it up with gravel and I rowed the thing back to the other end and somebody unloaded it. Here again, a fairly cushy job.

The Japs were not all that bad but it was about this time that the changeover came with Jap guards. They brought in Korean soldiers with Jap officers to replace the frontline troops.

These were a different class of people altogether. The Koreans hated the Japs and they all hated us. The officers were presumably of a class unfit for frontline service and didn't like the job they were doing, so things got a bit rough after that.

One of the officers in the house next to us had a habit that if he was in a bad mood he would walk up the frontline and kick us fellows in the shins.

Nothing you could do about it but that was the way it went.

A funny thing happened there. In between the changeover, all of the old guards disappeared one day. We woke up and there were no guards there. This went on for about four or five days until the new guards arrived. After a couple of days of this, I got a bright idea. We had with us a Sergeant who had been with us on guard duty at Kuala Lumpur and I put it to him, and he put it to the Officer. Why didn't we take half a dozen men and wander around town?

So, we all got dressed up. We borrowed proper clothes, boots, socks and we all put a red cross armband on our arms. Six of us plus the Sergeant formed up on the road outside the wire compound, and we marched straight down Lornie Road into the city and through to the Great World.

A lot of our other fellows were still there. The thing was that nobody challenged us.

We saw a few cars with Japs in them and if we did that, we gave a very smart eyes-right and the Sergeant saluted. We marched in step all the way.

We went into the Great World. Going through Chinatown on the way, the Chinese were very pleased to see us, and they loaded our packs up with food. So, we got into the Great World. They had plenty of food there and we loaded up and then marched all the way home again with not a blow struck. Everybody in our house ate pretty well that night.

Then all the guys in our house were transferred down the road about a quarter of a mile to an old wooden building. We didn't know why, but we were engaged in cleaning up exercises around the place. We were wandering around picking up this and that, not doing a hell of a lot really at all. Jimmy Arthur-Smith and Len and Dick Males and I built ourselves a lean-to in which we slept. We had rough bunks and were quite comfortable. Food wasn't all that bad.

AUSTRALIAN WAR MEMORIAL                                                      056555

*Figure 15: Australian Soldiers Posing with Shells*
*L-R Bofors Shell, 6lb Shell, 3.7" Anti-Aircraft*
*c. 1943. (AWM 056555)*

We had our own cookhouse nearby and one day while we were out on the working party, I picked up a Bofors shell *(a 40mm shell)*, obviously unfired. It was not in its brass case and was just the shell itself. I took it home and decided I wanted to see how this thing worked. So, I unscrewed the detonator top and pulled all that off and I figured out how all that operated.

On the base of the shell was this white substance. I couldn't figure out what it was, so I got a nail and was poking with it—and all of a sudden, *swoosh.*

What I had been poking at was the phosphorous type of stuff, the tracer element that enables you to see where the shell has gone after it's been fired.

This went off like a gigantic Roman candle. I have never seen anybody move so quickly. Jimmy and Len and Dick, one minute they were there and next minute they were out. But it didn't do any damage. It didn't explode or anything.

With this shell in my hand and this stuff streaming out the back of it for about four or five seconds, I was feeling an awful bloody fool, but no damage was done.

# HOSPITALISED

———— ◆ ◇ ◆ ————

S hortly thereafter, I contracted scrotal diphtheria[26] as we found out later. My testicles swelled up to the size of tennis balls and were covered with weeping sores. Very painful of course, and I was put on light duties; they put me into a building across the road which had been converted into a hospital. After about a week there, they sent me back to Roberts Hospital at Changi.

The treatment there consisted of scrubbing off all the sores back to the raw flesh and bathing them in a saline solution twice a day.

After a week of this, it started to clear up and I eventually recovered.

There was a lot of it going around, quite an epidemic of it. We were in an isolation ward and after I got back on my feet, I wasn't supposed to go outside. There was a message that came in that Johnny Bell was outside and wanted to see me. I walked out up into the main quadrangle in the middle of the hospital, found Johnny and we had a bit of a yarn. Then he went off and I didn't catch up with him until a couple of years later.

Anyway, I got caught and in due army procedure, I was paraded before the Commanding Officer of the hospital, being out

---

[26] A bacterial infection spread through human-to-human contact by coughs or sneezes.

of bounds from an isolation ward and I was fined 10 shillings which went into my pay book and all shows in my army records.

Having recovered from all this, I went back to the unit at Changi and I had only been there a week when I got up one morning and found something was wrong with my right leg.

I didn't seem to have any feeling in it, no power in it, so I reported sick.

AUSTRALIAN WAR MEMORIAL                                                    P02569.192

*Figure 16: POWs B Pearce (NXNX4417),*
*O Jackson (NX47506), unidentified, with Beriberi*
*c. 1943. (AWM P02569.192)*

The doc made a few tests and said, "You've got beriberi" which is a vitamin B1 deficiency. So, back into Roberts Hospital. I lost the use of my right leg and right arm—no feeling and no power in them, although the left leg and arm and everything else worked fine. It was caused by diet deficiencies which were the result of being so sick with diphtheria when I didn't eat.

The prescription was a better diet and three teaspoons full of Marmite per day for about two weeks. That's why I hate Marmite now, or Vegemite[27], but it cured me.

While I was in there, there was another chap who had a chess set and he taught me to play chess and I got quite interested and fairly proficient at it, but I wouldn't even know how to play the game now.

---

[27] Marmite and Vegemite, thick black spreads made from yeast extract, containing high concentrations of vitamin B.

# FROM SINGAPORE TO THAILAND

———— ◆ ◇ ◆ ————

S o, back to Selarang Square[28] at Changi, and this was about December/January 1943. Brigadier Frederick "Blackjack" Galleghan had taken charge of the place and he was a real nark, but he made a good soldier, though one who was strictly for the rules.

AUSTRALIAN WAR MEMORIAL                                    P00672.001

*Figure 17: Selarang Square c. 1942. (AWM P00672.001)*

The deal was that no one was to go outside the boundaries, which were all barbed wire, under any circumstances. Because every unit has

---

[28] Selarang Square was the site of revolt of British-Australian prisoners from August-September 1942. Known as the "Selarang Squeeze", four Australians who attempted to escape were executed. Lieutenant Galleghan was ordered by the Japanese to witness the executions. Under duress, all prisoners then signed a promise to not to attempt to escape.

got its series of entrepreneurs who run the two-up games and wheeling and dealing all over the place, Blackjack appointed us to guard the known exits from the compound. There were gates at various places around the whole thing.

Changi village was only a quarter of a mile down the road.

I was on duty at one of these gates one night.

Our instructions were that nobody was to go out or come in. Of course, this was a big joke. Three or four blokes went out with packs on their backs and kit bags under their arms and an hour later, they came back. And as they came back, they appeared from nowhere. They could move very quietly and as they went past, they thrust a great bag of tobacco in our hands.

That's what they were doing. They were going out, buying tobacco and selling it. Doing very nicely too but, so much for Blackjack's "Nobody goes in or out."

I got enough tobacco that one night to keep me going for nearly six months. It was a wonderful thing as far as I was concerned.

In March 1943, we set out for Thailand.

The total going up in this group was something like 5,000 of which—2,200 I believe—were Australians. I was with U Battalion on D Force. Our CO (*Commanding Officer*) was Captain Reg Newton and U Battalion was comprised of some 300 2/19th and 200 2/20th men and officers.

We went by train and had to carry sufficient rations with us to see us through the train journey. The carriages we travelled in were rice trucks, each about eighteen feet long, seven feet tall and seven feet wide—thirty men to a truck.

These were completely enclosed with steel topsides and a door on either side.

During the day they were stinking hot, and at nighttime, quite cold.

If you wanted to go to the toilet while the train was on the move, you had to go out through the door and we could not all lie down together.

We had to take it in turns to lie down, sit down or stand up.

I seem to remember we took about three days on that journey. We stopped several times, once at Kuala Lumpur, another time at Penang, then up on the border. Water was our main trouble because Captain Newton kept drumming into us that you didn't drink water unless it had been boiled. That wasn't always possible, and a few stomach upsets occurred on en route.

We arrived in Thailand at Ban Pong which was a staging camp run by the British. We stayed there for one night only and then moved on to Tha Sao (*also known as Tarsao*), this time going by train because the railway line had been built almost as far as Tha Sao, almost outside the camp.

Tha Sao was, at that stage, a hospital camp and we settled in there in tents. Japanese tents, not very good ones, but at least they kept most of the water out.

We liked to build beds which consisted of bamboo slats stretched out on top of a bamboo framework, two feet from the ground—which meant that you could sleep quite comfortably on there. I think that we had twelve men in a tent—pretty crowded.

Tha Sao was situated right on the riverbank so there was no shortage of water. Our cookhouses were set up on the riverbank too, and we got ourselves fairly well organised.

# THE THAI-BURMA RAILWAY

———— ◆ ◇ ◆ ————

O ur work parties here were out on the railway line, which was slowly passing by, and our job was to clear the track through the scrub, level it out and clear it away—pick and shovel work. After that, the next team would put down ballast and then one after that would put down the sleepers. Then the rail cars would come up behind with the rail tracks on them, and a laying gang would put then down and spike them in. I noticed when we saw some of these rails, practically every one that I saw was labelled 'BHP made in Australia'[29].

Whilst we had been overnight at Ban Pong, I was walking back from the river after I had a wash and a stray dog came out and bit me on the leg.

This turned into a tropical ulcer and I was put on light duties for a few days.

On one of these days, half a dozen of us were sent up to the Japanese Hospital on the outskirts of the camp on emu parade (*picking up papers, cleaning up*) and generally staying out of trouble.

Whilst I was there, a bee or wasp stung me in the left eye and in a matter of a few minutes, the eye was closed, and the whole

---

[29] An Australian multinational natural resources company, historically known for steel products. Now trading as BHP Billiton.

thing was puffed up and quite sore. There was nothing I could do about it and I was working near a tent and a Jap officer came out.

As instructed, I came to attention and he walked over to me and said, "You have problems."

I said, "Yes, sir. A wasp has stung me."

He said, "Come with me."

He took me into the tent. He was a doctor.

He spoke perfect English with a pronounced Australian accent. And he put an injection into me that eased the pain, washed the eye out and put a big wad of cotton wool over and bandaged it in place. All this time he was talking, and he asked me where I came from— and I said I came from Cremorne, Sydney. "Ah," he said, "I used to live at Cremorne."

When I was a lad going to school at Cremorne, Neutral Bay, there was an enormous great house right opposite the tram line at Military Road on the lower side of Cremorne, towards the water on the corner. It was a very luxurious place, and this was where a Japanese family lived.

This doctor told me this was where he lived. It was quite a coincidence.

He said amongst other things, not to worry, and that after the war, we'd find it exactly as was. He indicated the Japanese didn't want to capture Australia. They wanted the East Indies where the oil was, that they wanted rubber—and most of all, they wanted India.

It was the jewel of the East and this was the whole idea of the railway. They wanted to supply their troops who were attacking through Burma, and they wanted to capture India.

The speedo (*an eighteen-hour workday, derived from the Japanese Guards commanding 'Supīdo', translation speed*) works started about now. The day started at daybreak when we got up and had breakfast which was usually boiled rice, with perhaps some greens. Then it was check parade when heads were counted, and then to work half a mile away. Most of the work here was making cuttings, moving dirt and we worked in teams of four. And we had to move one cubic metre of dirt per man, per day. There were two digging, one with a pick, one with a shovel and two carting dirt away in rattan baskets. We swapped around of course. The only problem was that the shovels were made from old forty-four-gallon drums and they were pretty useless. The picks had no temper in them, and they were not much better. The result was that we didn't get through the job as quickly as we should have at times, and a few bamboo sticks were wielded by the guards.

About this time, Reg Newton[30] had come to an agreement with Boon Pong[31].

He was a Thai trader who had a fleet of boats that ran up and down the river, and he had a contract with the Jap camps for food, including our food of course.

Reg came to an agreement with Boon Pong whereby he supplied us under the table without the Japs' knowledge, with medical supplies, extra food, etc.

Reg arranged to issue him with cheques drawn on his bank in Sydney which could be presented after the war.

---

[30] Lieutenant Colonel Reginald Newton MBE OBE ED NX34734, known for his leadership while a POW.
[31] Boonpong Sirivejjabhandu 21.4.1906-29.01.1982 a Thai Merchant and part of the Thai resistance.

This actually happened and the amount was eventually refunded to Reg by the Army.

The Japs were paying us—I think it was about 5c. per person per day. Reg took charge of all this money which was used to buy openly some medical supplies and amenities for us. We could get an issue of tobacco when we needed it, which was very handy.

Cigarette papers were of course, off-limits.

We used up every bit of paper we could find and eventually, I personally made myself a pipe out of bamboo and used that for the rest of the period.

At the end of the day's work, we marched back to camp about dusk. And the first thing—and this was a feature of every camp we were in where it was possible—everyone took off to the river for a swim and a wash. This was a daily routine which was very rarely not done.

After that came the evening meal and we would wander around the camp or sit in the tents and talk. There was no light of course, except some fellows arranged to make lamps.

A metal container, for example, the bottom of a drink can filled with palm oil and with a wick in it. It gave off a bit of light.

This was the wet season which lasted up until October/November. It rained almost every day and dirt roads all through the camp and out of the camp were usually ankle-deep in mud.

Now that we had a little bit better food, the Jap rations had increased slightly and although we weren't well fed and were always hungry, we had sufficient to keep us going. The biggest problem was diseases such as malaria, amoebic dysentery and probably the worst of all, tropical ulcers. We had no proper medical supplies.

Sulphanilamide *(an antibacterial powder)* was known to us, but our stores had run out. We had Doc *(David Clive Anthony)* Hinder[32] with very few instruments and almost nothing with which to counteract dysentery and particularly the ulcers. These would, in the climate there, eat a man's leg away until the bone was evident and in lots of cases, the doctors had no option other than to amputate.

Fortunately, they were able to get supplies of chloroform.

This was the pattern throughout the whole of our time on the line, active participation in heavy work. After about a month at Tha Sao, we moved to a camp at North Tha Sao. We had to carve a campsite out of the jungle not far from the river and we were in tents there. We didn't stay there all that long, and we moved farther up the line to South Ton Chan. This would have been about the 150k mark from Ban Pong which was the base of the line.

---

[32] Captain David Clive Critchley Hinder (Medical Officer) NX76302.

AUSTRALIAN WAR MEMORIAL 157859

*Figure 18: Hellfire Pass, also known as*
*Konyu or K3 c. 1945. (AWM 157859)*

At South Ton Chan, we were camped on the edge of a beautiful crystal-clear stream that ran down from the hills behind us. The whole of these sites were surrounded by mountains and hills. The roughest-looking country you ever saw in your life.

We weren't allowed to drink it unboiled, but we did wash in it every day. The Japs had the camp on the other side of the stream, and they kept out of our road and we kept out of theirs.

Not long after getting there, I kicked and broke my toe on a tent peg and this caused me a bit of trouble for a few weeks until it healed up.

Then a major catastrophe happened.

The Japs brought probably a couple of hundred Chinese coolie *(labourer)* workers and they camped up on the other side of the creek about 150 yards away.

These poor beggars had no organisation. They didn't have our experience in these conditions, or someone like Reg to look after them, and in no time at all disease was evident there, not only dysentery but with the wet season, cholera.

Cholera was a waterborne disease and in a matter of a month, every one of those poor devils had died. Then one or two of our fellows caught cholera and within two weeks, we had lost twenty men. Cholera was very sudden. It could take you out in about two to three days.

Our Camp Commandant was a Japanese Warrant Officer Hiramatsu[33]. He became known as the tiger of the line. He was a big heavy tough guy and a strict disciplinarian, and life was pretty miserable under him.

At this camp, we were making cuttings through rock outcrops up on the line and of course, no proper drills. We did it with what was called the hammer and tap, a long drill about two feet long with a sharpened end; one man held the drill and the other bloke belted it with a sledgehammer. It was slow work. We had to do one man, one metre of drill hole per day.

We were working in an area about, I suppose, thirty or forty yards square, and when the holes were dug, the Jap engineers would come along and put down a plug of gelignite with a detonator and a fuse attached. The fuse stuck out of the ground and when all these were set in place, probably half a dozen or ten of us were given a piece of proper match rope which was glowing on one end and each man had to light five fuses.

---

[33] After the war, Warrant Office Aitaro Hiramatsu was prosecuted as a war criminal and sentenced to death.

I was one of them, and the rest of the mob sheltered about fifty or sixty yards away behind a great outcrop of rock. The thing was when everybody started, I had a bit of trouble getting my fuses lit and all of a sudden, I got the last one going and looked up, and I was the last one left. Everyone else was gone and I was surrounded by about 150 sticks of gelignite with fuses burning down them.

I must have covered fifty yards to the rock column in Olympic time. I dived over the top just as the whole bang lot went up. Of course, all the boys thought it was very funny, but at the time I wasn't very amused. In hindsight, it was a rather amusing incident.

It was here that I had my first attack of malaria. The previous year, when Johnny Bell had visited me in the isolation ward at Roberts Hospital at Selerang, he'd given me a diary, a large book about A4 size, properly bound and I kept that diary until it was stolen from me by the Japs about eighteen months later.

I seem to remember I recorded about sixty or seventy attacks of malaria up to that time. It came around quite regularly BT (*Benign Tertian*[34]) type, every thirteen days and lasted about two to three days, and then repeated itself. This happened right through to the end of the war and then back into civilian life, when I had a couple of attacks.

South Ton Chan was, I am sure, the worst camp I was in. It was away from the river and all supplies had to come by road, if you could call it a road, through the jungle. Japanese trucks tried to carry them up.

The mud was anything from ankle to knee-deep. It rained all the time and we spent a lot of our nighttime when we were supposed to be

---

[34] BT, Benign Tertian malaria is characterised by fever that occurs every 3rd day. It has a low mortality rate.

sleeping, going back down the muddy road and carrying the supplies on our shoulders because the trucks got bogged.

With the cholera outbreak, we couldn't use the stream for bathing anymore and our cooks did a marvellous job of boiling water. And when we came back from the day's work, each man was given a billy can full of boiled water in which he had to wash.

The result was that we were never clean. We were always muddy.

We had the pleasure here of seeing the Japanese frontline troops march through to Burma along the railway line. The railway hadn't actually arrived where we were, as we were still getting the track ready. But they followed the path of it, carrying all their goods on their backs and in small trolley carts and they even were driving the odd bullock with them. They were doing it the hard way, in the mud, too.

# TON CHAN, THAILAND

———————— ◆ ◇ ◆ ————————

A fter a couple of months—it was now about June/July 1943—
we moved to Central Ton Chan, about twenty kilometres on.
The camp here was built on a small plateau about 400 yards
from the river and supplies could now come through by barge.

Reg had organised our money supplies to buy goods from Boon
Pong and we found that the standard of food we were getting, thanks
to Reg, was improving while it still wasn't good tucker.

There were a large number of British in this camp and their
Officers were absolute no-hopers.

The British Army Officers and enlisted men didn't mix at all, so
the result was that the poor enlisted men were not getting as much care
and attention from their officers as ours did.

It was here that the boots began to give me and a lot of others some
trouble; the new boots that we'd worn when we left Selarang were now
history, and a lot of us, including me, were going around without
boots. The Japanese then issued us with their own type of boot called
a track boot, made of rubber sole, canvas top.

The only trouble was that the largest Japanese soldier was about
an eight and I took a size ten. We overcame the problem by cutting the
top out of the canvas part of the boot around the toe, allowing my foot
to hang over the sole by an inch or two and to stop the sole flapping
around, I tied it with a piece of wire back to my toe onto the canvas

upper. This way for the rest of our prisoner of war period, I managed to keep myself in some sort of footwear.

The railway had passed through Ton Chan by now and our job was maintenance, ballasting, repairing bridges and collecting wood for the engines. The real speedo work had slowed down a lot and we were not working as hard as we used to. We quite often got a Sunday off and we spent the time down in the river, washing ourselves and our clothes.

To take up some of our spare time, if there was much, the Japs decided that we would learn their drill. We were told how to march in Japanese, how to turn in Japanese and how to number in Japanese. All of our troops had, for quite a long time now, been compelled to salute every Japanese we saw, regardless of his rank. If you failed to do so, you got a bashing.

We built our own attap huts at Ton Chan, a fair way from the British. We got on well with the British troops, but we had no time for their officers. I remember one Yasumi (*Japanese, translation rest day*), we were all down in the river, the Kwai Noi.

It flowed very quickly there, and there was a bay probably 100 yards or so long, and the water flowed back into this bay quite slowly, a good place to swim.

We were there one day, and the Japs decided they would get some fish. So, they went up the river about 300 or 400 yards, and they tossed in quite a lot of sticks of gelly (*gelignite*). A lot of big bangs and the Japs were rushing around down the river, trying to find the fish which should have been stunned and would have floated to the surface. When we were swimming and standing in the fairly shallow water in this bay, we found that hundreds and hundreds of fish were washing in, not on the surface, but on the bottom. So we continued to wash ourselves and most of us had three or four fish stuck in the crotch of our shorts, or we were standing on them or held them in bags on the bottom of the river with our feet on top of the bags. The Japanese got some fish, but we sure got a lot in our meal that night too.

We were out on the job one day on the jungle track, and we were having lunch.

Snow White[35] was sitting next to me and I looked down the road and saw a tiger walk out of the jungle on the track about 150 yards away. It appeared to be a young tiger, not terribly large, but big enough. The Jap guard there was only a blooming kid and he had a Japanese rifle, a small-calibre, high-velocity thing.

We called him over and in great excitement pointed down—*tiger, tiger, tiger!*

"Oh," he said, and he walked down and tried to bag this tiger with his rifle. We were only hoping that he would walk into the mother tiger or father tiger because his rifle against a tiger would be quite useless. However, the tiger disappeared, and no harm was done either way.

Another time, we were out in a similar area and out of the bush staggered one of these bullocks that the Japanese had been taking up to Burma with them for food. Poor devil of a thing, it was only skin and bone and could barely walk. It wandered out onto the clearing and the Jap guard there had a .303 rifle and he put about three bullets into the poor beast, and it was still standing on its feet.

So, I walked over to the guard. Most of these guards were only kids and this one was a youngster too. I, by sign language, persuaded him to give me the rifle which he did, and I put one through the

---

[35] Possibly Milton Thomas "Snow" Fairclough WX2629.

bullock's head right between the eyes. We all had a little bit of meat that night too, the Japs as well.

Our butchers used to do all the butchering if there was going to be any meat in camp, and they were always very careful to see that we got the best cuts.

# A POW CHRISTMAS

— ◆ ◇ ◆ —

It was now around October 1943, and we moved farther up the line about ten or twelve kilometres to Tampi (*Tampines*). Here, we built our huts again and this was a much cleaner camp than Ton Chan, not so far from the river and maintenance work on the line.

The Jap Commander known as the Tiger had become a lot more amenable, thanks very largely to the efforts of Reg Newton and the fact that the line had been completed up as far as he was concerned and all we had to do was keep it open. We had more time off and we weren't working such long hours, but we were still getting the odd bashing here and there.

*Figure 19: Hintok Tampi Bridge*
*(Hellfire Pass in the background) c. 1945. (AWM 120509)*

It came Christmas time in Tampi, and Reg persuaded the Tiger to allow us to put on not only a Christmas Dinner, but also a pantomime and entertainment. Using funds saved up from our Japanese pay, and with the help of Boon Pong, considerable rations were purchased for the big dinner and we really had full bellies on that day. The Japs agreed to allow us to put on a pantomime. I didn't take part in it, but the fellows did a good job.

They built a stage and put on Cinderella, well, *their* version of Cinderella anyway.

There were three ugly sisters, Reg Newton, Captain (*Keith*) Westbrook, and Doc (*David*) Hinder. Now it was a real riot. There were some British in camp with us and boxing matches were arranged too. A ring was erected in the middle of the compound and several matches took place. One particular guy from the British Forces, a West Indian, was a really good boxer.

I remember him.

Another thing, too, was at the conclusion of the whole thing on Christmas night, one of the British produced a violin. It was a full moon almost that night, and I can always remember this guy standing in the middle of the boxing ring playing most beautifully on this violin.

He was a very talented player.

It was about this time that I had a lot of malaria, some dysentery and my bronchitis was starting to give me trouble, so Doc Hinder decided I should go back to Tha Sao Hospital Camp. I didn't want to leave, but he was the boss and I did what I was told. A number of us went back down there.

AUSTRALIAN WAR MEMORIAL                                        P00761 011

*Figure 20: Four prisoners of war (POWs) with*
*beriberi in Tha Sao Hospital Camp. (AWM P00761.011)*

It also had been the original base camp when we'd first come up to the country. It was now a hospital camp, dirty and we were all mixed up. We weren't with our own unit fellows at all, but we were put into wards according to what disease we had and there were a lot of Australians there. It was a case of making acquaintances there all over again.

The first thing I did at Tha Sao was to contract scabies, a disease caused by mites that breed in dirty conditions. I had festering sores all over both my arms and there was no treatment that they had that would do anything for it, until one day, an Asian doctor, not one of the Japanese, came around and produced a hypodermic syringe, a needle I think a veterinarian would have used, and he took two big syringes of blood out of each of my arms and gave it back to me in my buttocks.

An experiment, he said. Well within three days, my scabies were starting to disappear and within a week, they were gone completely. I don't know even now if it was a local treatment or something out of our own medical books. It worked.

A chap I had palled up with there in the same hut went out on a working party in the Japanese food stores. He said, *I know where there is an awful lot of sugar to be had quite easily.* So we went to work quickly and borrowed two kerosene tins and that night, a very dark night, we sent out on a raid of the Japs' stores. We just got through the bamboo fence around the compound and all of a sudden, the lights went on and there was a Jap guard screaming out "Kura! Kura!" (*Japanese, translation storehouse*) and we scarpered very smartly back through the hole in the fence.

We scuttled back to our own hut, threw the tins under the bamboo beds and then pulled the blanket over us. When the Jap guards came through looking for someone, we were all snoring soundly, thank goodness.

It was in Tha Sao, that I first came across the treatment that was used for tropical ulcers. I am not sure whether it was (*Ernest*) Weary Dunlop[36] or Albert Coates[37] or who it was that designed this, but it was very efficient. What they did was, they sharpened spoons—teaspoons or dessertspoons—until their edges were like razors and with that, they scraped all the ulcerated flesh and the clean flesh right down until there was nothing left of the disease.

No local anaesthetic was used, and we sat on each leg and an orderly held onto each arm, and a piece of bamboo was put between the patient's teeth.

---

[36] Colonel Sir Ernest Edward "Weary" Dunlop AC CMG OBE an Australian surgeon, known for his leadership while a POW.
[37] Lieutenant Colonel Sir Albert Coates an Australian surgeon, a fellow POW, and a mentor to "Weary" Dunlop.

This worked well with the smaller ulcers, but of course, the bigger ones that chewed right through to the bone were untreatable and, in most cases, the limb had to be amputated.

The biggest problem with Tha Sao at that time was boredom. There were no working parties except cleanup around the camp. Nothing to do, and the other big problem was amoebic dysentery. We never struck any cholera in any camp I was at after South Ton Chan. But amoebic dysentery became the big killer. There was very little in the way of proper medications to treat it and the death toll was quite heavy.

# THA MUANG

———— ◆ ◇ ◆ ————

After a month or two at Tha Sao—this would be early 1944—the team I was with was moved back to Tha Muang, another light duties camp, not far from Kanchanaburi. This was a very clean camp and there was no hard work, but the Jap guards and the Jap Commander were particularly brutal bastards. The Jap Commander was a young fellow, looked about twelve years old, and dressed like a proud peacock. We dubbed him Boy Shoko[38].

He was a particularly nasty type.

He would bung on check parades in the middle of the night just for the heck of it.

I can remember one day, for some reason, the entire camp was paraded in the middle of the compound with several thousand men, and he kept us sitting there all day in the sun. No food, no water, no nothing, until about ten o'clock that night. Not long after that, the rest of the battalion came back from Tampi and we became a complete unit again.

Taking stock of my own possessions at that time, I had no shirt and no shorts, and I covered myself with a lap-lap *(a type of loincloth)* and a pair of Japanese rubber boots, no hat. I had a blanket, an army issue pack, and a water bottle. Inside the pack, I

---

[38] Lieutenant Kishio Usuki, also known as the "Konyu Kid". He was sentenced to death after the war for his brutal treatment of POWs.

had a mess tin and spoon, an ordinary table knife that I sharpened up to use as a razor for shaving every now and then, a small tin with some personal belongings I still maintained including my one or two photographs I'd brought from home, and my diary which I still wrote up every day or two.

It was unfortunate that late in 1944, the Japs put on a search while we were out on a working party somewhere and they took the diary. I was a bit worried after that, that they would sit down and read it because there were some very uncomplimentary things in it.

There were no repercussions from that.

*Figure 21: B-24 Liberator Bomber. (AWM AC0079)*

By now, we were seeing a bit of British Air Force activity. Bomber planes would fly over, usually at nighttime and at a great height. At Tha Muang one day, one of these Liberators came over. He would only be 300–400 feet up. You could see the gunners in the blister and the tail gunner quite clearly. He didn't have his bomb bay doors open, so he was only on a recon flight and there was a big Japanese petrol dump only a mile or two from our camp.

But a Japanese guard on the perimeter of our camp got the bright idea. He had the Japanese rifle which was like a pea shooter. He took a shot at the plane as it went over and a couple of seconds later, the tail gunner turned on him with a bzzz brrrr.

Exit one Jap guard. That tail gunner was a hell of a good shot.

Some of the fellows that rejoined us at this camp were Bill Saunderson, Ken Sweet, Harry Simister, Mac Watts and Snow White. At nighttime in the huts, there was very little light except for the odd oil lamp, and Kenny Sweet and I used to start an argument just to keep ourselves in trim. We both knew Sydney very, very well and we started arguments just about where one street ran or what suburb was next to another, silly damned things and we would go on for an hour or more, arguing backwards and forth, but it kept the mind going. The mob got sick of it and they would say, "Oh shut up" and we all went to sleep.

I forgot when previously listing my total assets, that I had one blanket.

At this time, Tha Muang was a final concentration-like camp entailing all the work parties that had come up or were coming down from the line. The line was finished, and all the work parties were brought back to Tha Muang where a large hospital section was put up. The camp consisted of Australians, British, Dutch— but mainly British, and the British were in charge of it. Weary Dunlop was the Chief Medical Officer at this camp. Our officers were (*Reg)* Newton, (*Keith)* Westbrook and (*Ralph)* Sanderson.

A team of us was sent very high up the line. We travelled by train. I can remember there was Bill Saunderson, Macky Watts, Ken Sweet, and we went to a camp called Lin Thin.

We established our own camp there and we were under tents on the river. A special job: a railway bridge over a cutting had subsided. The piles holding the thing up had not been put down to a sufficient depth and when a heavy rail engine went over it, it sort-of sagged in the middle. Our job was to repair it. Although there was a bit of speedo, this camp was actually quite a good one. We built it ourselves and there were probably only about a hundred of us there. The food was quite good and the Japanese not all that bad to get on with.

We were there for about a month, I think, and nothing special happened at that camp although one thing I do remember. We were walking out one morning to work, and we walked past the edge of a cutting. It had been cut through the normal soil and had banks on either side, of clay. I suppose from the top of one bank to the top of the other was thirty-five to forty feet. It rained the night before and the banks were all quite smooth except that on the far bank opposite us where I was walking, there was one footprint of a tiger. How the hell that tiger got across that thirty-foot jump and left only one footprint, I never could figure out.

# THE THREE PAGODAS

——————— ◆ ◇ ◆ ———————

We moved back to Tha Muang about the middle of 1944, and in June of that year, the POWs being transported to Japan were selected. Newton and Sanderson were sent together with about 1,500 men, of which a couple of hundred were 2/19th.

I was on the sick list at the time with dysentery and I stayed behind. Our officer left behind was Captain Westbrook, and I think Lieutenant Frank Ramsbotham of the 2/20th stayed behind with us.

Our working parties in the camp were still kept up.

We went outside the camp occasionally to work at the Japanese store dumps and particularly the Japanese petrol dumps, an enormous area of forty-four-gallon drums of aviation fuel.

What it was wanted for up there, we never found out because they didn't have an awful lot of trucks; the trains burnt wood and there was no airfield nearby.

One job we had at Tha Muang was to build an enormous moat right around the camp. This was about twelve feet deep and about twenty feet wide and its object was not clear to us at that time, although subsequently, we found out it was going to be used to exterminate the entire camp.

They had machine gun nests set up all around the perimeter overlooking this trench, and we were quite sure that had the order been given later on, as the war got closer to an end, prisoners were to be eliminated completely and the trench would have held them all and nobody would have known anything about it. Or that was what the Japanese thought anyway.

By now, in July/August 1944, the line was virtually finished, and all the camps had been brought back down to the low country. Tha Sao was the hospital camp.

Tha Muang was partly hospital, partly another camp. Nakhon Pathom had been established as a hospital camp not far from Bangkok.

*Figure 22: POW Hospital/Surgery at*
*Nakom Pathom c. 1944. (AWM 157874)*

Maintenance teams were being sent up the line from time to time to carry out repairs, and about September, a team of us, probably 100, went up to Nieke. This was almost onto the Burma border, not far from the Three Pagodas Pass.

AUSTRALIAN WAR MEMORIAL · 157865

*Figure 23: Aparon, Three Pagodas Pass, Thailand. (AWM 157865)*

We travelled by train, lying on flat tops with all the other merchandise that the Japs were sending up there. The trip took about, I think, two to three days. We were up there to cut wood for the locomotives; there wasn't any coal, so teams were all over the place, cutting timber and packing it on the side of the line at various sidings.

The camp we took over was a standard bamboo hut with attap roofs and bamboo beds. We had platforms. Only trouble was, the hut had been previously occupied, and it wasn't left terribly clean, and it was crawling with bugs of all sorts. But the work wasn't too bad there, and the Japs weren't hard to get on with. The food was fairly plentiful.

Each man had to cut a pile of one cubic metre of firewood per day, cut into half-metre lengths. There were teams out in the jungle, felling the trees.

The Thais had the elephants, which would bring them in.

It was amazing to see how the elephants could handle these gigantic logs. They would pick them up like matchsticks and pile them exactly where they were supposed to be.

We had teams sawing them into lengths and other teams splitting. I was with a team of three. I think Snow White was one of them and it was quite cold up there. We were very high up in the mountains, terribly rugged country. At nighttime, we would light fires in the alleyway down the centre of the hut to keep ourselves warm.

At this time of the year, the rainy season had finished and with winter coming on, the weather was pretty dry but at nighttime, quite cold. We even had frosts sometimes.

We had been there for perhaps three weeks when the Sergeant sleeping in the bunk opposite me suddenly became ill with a fever. The next afternoon, I helped bury him.

All of a sudden, the camp was overtaken with this illness and nobody knew what it was at the time, but we found out later it was typhus[39]. Typhus was a pretty serious thing without proper medication; we had a doctor in camp with us and a few medical orderlies, but not much in the way of drugs. Typhus could be very deadly, and it was almost as bad as cholera.

---

[39] Typhus is an infectious disease, even over 50 years since the end of WWII there is no vaccine available.

AUSTRALIAN WAR MEMORIAL                    P00762.001

*Figure 24: Members of the British military carry the*
*coffin of Warrant Officer Waldo (NX28141) who died of typhus,*
*5th December 1941. (AWM P00762.001)*

I can remember getting up in the middle of one night to go outside to the toilet, and the next thing I recall, I was lying back on my bunk. I'd apparently passed out. The boys brought me back in and laid me down and I got the fever. I can remember it was far worse than malaria, and I became disoriented and didn't know where I was or what I was doing. The last thing I can remember was Macky Watts[40] coming up and giving me what we called quinine bombs.

Macky had some quinine wrapped up in a little piece of cigarette paper and you swallowed it—vile-tasting stuff.

---

[40] There were a three Private Watts that were POWs at the same time as Bill and in the same or neighbouring units. In the 2/19th William George Watts (NX35513), in the 2/18th Ernest Watts (NX27432), and Ellis Roy Watts (NX32277). The latter, Ellis, died in Borneo 17.6.1945. It is possible that one of them had the nickname "Mac", but this is not confirmed.

I didn't really think that quinine did much for typhus, but Macky was trying anyway.

After that, I passed out and I learned later that I had become delirious and unconscious, and I was like that for two to three days.

When I woke up, I was in a different hut, the fever was gone, the head fairly clear.

I was lying on the bamboo bed and I got up on my elbows and looked around, and there were half a dozen dead bodies lined up near me. At that moment, an orderly walking past said, "Hey, that one moved." *That one* was me and I found that I was in the camp morgue.

Anyway, the orderly said, "Look sport, there's a train down at the siding waiting to go south; if you can get down there, get on it."

So, I took my pack and water bottle, which was all I had. That was the point where I lost my blanket because somewhere along the line, my blanket disappeared.

I crawled most of the way, a couple of hundred yards down to the siding.

There were the usual steel rice trucks there and fellows sitting in them and somebody grabbed me and got me into the truck. After a while the train took off. I wasn't in the mood to care where it was going or what I did, as long as I was doing something. We travelled most of that day, and that night we stopped off at Hintok. There were still some maintenance crews around and we spent the night at Hintok, and the following day got on another train and went for a couple more days down to Tha Makhan.

# THA MAKHAN CAMP

$\bullet \Diamond \bullet$

Tha Makhan (*also known as Tha Makham and Tamarkan*) was a camp which was then almost next door to the bridge they call 'the bridge on the River Kwai', the steel bridge which ran across the lower reaches of the Khwae Yai River. At the present time, it is quite a tourist attraction, they tell me. But there was a fairly large camp there and a hospital. I got in there and the MO (*Medical Officer*) came around, had a look at me and there was not much he could do.

I was over the fever and lucky to be alive and that was good.

*Figure 25: POWs sleeping in an attap hut. (AWM P01502.003)*

The food in the camp was quite good. There were no working parties and the Japs didn't worry us very much. That night, I heard some of our own fellows were there and those who had been up the line with us—Bill Saunderson and Sweety and Macky Watts, etc. They had all come back.

I wandered over to another hut and there were Bill Saunderson and Ken Sweet playing cards with an oil lamp between them. Bill Saunderson, who had a dark complexion, well I walked up and tapped him on the shoulder, and I said, "Hi, Bill." He looked up and I swear he turned white. He dropped his cards and said, "Shit, Lofty, I thought you were dead."

Next to the bridge at Tha Makhan, there were about three Jap anti-aircraft guns. I presumed they realised the bridge would be a prime target for bombs. Planes used to go over every night on their way down south somewhere to bomb somebody, we didn't know what. They were British planes of course, very high up. The Japs would always let off half a dozen rounds from the ack-ack guns. They never hit anything because they couldn't see what they were shooting at, and after they had let off half a dozen rounds, they would all scream out "Banzai! Banzai!" (*Long live the Emporer, a blessing for the Emperor of Japan*) and send us back to bed.

Late one afternoon, a plane came down.

It was very difficult to bomb that bridge because it was in between two very tall mountains, and the only way they could do it would be to come down the river which wasn't all that wide. That was what this plane did. We didn't hear it. It came down with its engines switched down low and probably only 500-600 feet up. It was a Liberator and it dropped, I think, three or four bombs. They wiped out the ack-ack guns, but unfortunately, one bomb dropped into our camp, right on top of a tent and about twenty-five of the guys bought it—pity *(29<sup>th</sup> November 1944)*[41].

Of course, there is always something funny happening in war, and I can remember the Jap guard who was wandering around the compound. He was very sloppily dressed.

He had on a pair of flip-flops and a rough old uniform with the normal cap they wear, and he was carrying a .303 rifle. After the bombing was over and we had all got to our feet again, you could see on the ground, first of all, the rifle, then his cap, and then his flip-flops—and he was long gone. He shot through. I don't know where he went to, but I can imagine he would have been in a bit of trouble with his officers after that one.

We stayed at Tha Makhan, I suppose, about two weeks. The food was fairly good there and I built up a bit of condition again, and then we were sent back to Tha Muang. The 2/19<sup>th</sup> and 2/20<sup>th</sup>, the new battalion boys were starting to be recalled to make a unit again. We had all been split up all over the place and now we were back in one heap. Apart from those of course, who had—in June— been sent to Japan. We had lost our officers as they had been taken away from us earlier in the year.

---

[41] On 29<sup>th</sup> November 1944, twenty-one planes bombed the area and four dropped on the camp, killing eighteen POW and wounding thirty-seven.

# CHRISTMAS IN THA MUANG

———— ◆ ◇ ◆ ————

As I remember, Weary Dunlop had become the Camp Commandant at Camp Tha Muang. I can remember being in Tha Muang at Christmas time and the cooks did a hell of a good job. The officers had saved up the money the Japs were paying us and with the Japs' permission, they had been able to buy extra rations here and there.

They had even set up in camp a little shop, and every now and then we would be issued with a token representing X number of dollars and cents, not very much. We could buy things in the shop. You could buy cigarettes and tobacco and you could even buy sweets there.

Some of the enterprising characters around the place went into making coffee. They would make coffee in four-gallon kerosene tins and cart it around at nighttime, and you could buy a cup of coffee for, I think, 5c. Although nobody had very much money.

That Christmas, we did fairly well. We ate fairly well.

I had another run-in with dysentery about this time, and I had been quite lucky because I got over it fairly easily, but after I got home, I was still carrying amoebic dysentery inside me.

I was in hospital in Sydney for five or six weeks while they got rid of it.

We did some working parties outside the camp, nothing terribly heavy, although the Japs were fair bastards. I remember one time we were around in the Japanese petrol dump—an enormous dump they had covering acres of ground. We were putting up camouflage nets and splashing tar and creosote all over them and, of course, we all got tar and creosote over our hands and arms and at knock-off time, one of the Japs produced a can of petrol.

I washed my hands and arms in this to take the creosote off, but of course, that was a mistake because this was high octane aviation fuel. I burnt them very badly and had blisters all over them, and I was out of action for several weeks.

Conditions in Tha Muang were, by comparison with the rest of the line, quite easy. Food was quite good, and the biggest problem was a lack of medical supplies. We still didn't have anything adequate to take care of any serious illness. I remember Bill Saunderson caught Blackwater Fever (*a complication of malaria*) and we all thought he was going to cark it, but he didn't.

Tough old beggar was Bill.

At nighttime after the evening meal, half a dozen of us used to sit out in the cool and we would yarn about this, that and the other and the talk invariably got back to what you would do when you got home. Everybody said, "Well, the first thing I am going to do is have a good feed." And then we would all say what we were going to eat and what was our favourite food.

We'd spend several hours out there doing nothing but wishful thinking. We didn't know when we were going to get home. We knew that there were radios in the camp, but nobody ever told us particularly what was going on, because it would have been dangerous to do so. Somebody would have blabbed, and the Japs would have found out there was a radio. The officers knew what was going on and of course, they knew best.

# ON TO BANGKOK

———————— ◆ ◇ ◆ ————————

About March 1945, a team of some fifty of us was loaded onto a train, still in the old rice-carrying carriages, and we travelled towards Bangkok.

Tha Muang was about seventy or eighty miles or so from Bangkok.

The country around there was getting more closely settled—no jungle, just farming land with small villages everywhere.

As we approached Bangkok, it was quite amazing to see civilisation again after two years out of sight completely. There were houses and gardens and people walking around.

We stopped in Bangkok at the lower end on the western side of the river. Not far away, there was a substantial steel bridge with several arches in it crossing the river; it was mainly for vehicular traffic. One of the arches was lined with the term 'out of action' on the riverbank.

We found out later the British had said to the Thais, "Either you put the bridge out of action or we will with our bombs," so the Thais took one of the arches out.

We travelled past Bangkok and around to a waterfront docks area several kilometres out of the town, and on the river not far from the main seaway. Obviously, the actual dock area was where seagoing vessels pulled in. We were camped in one of these go-downs which was empty, and about 400 yards farther on, there were substantial buildings occupied by Japanese.

We didn't know what this was, and we couldn't have cared less really.

We spent about three days there and one afternoon, an air raid alarm went.

P00502.001

*Figure 26: The Bridge over the river Kwai,*
*severely damaged by aerial bombing. (AWM P00502.001)*

We could see three planes—we learnt later they were B29's. They were so high up that all you could see were the vapour trails. They'd have to have been about 40,000 feet up. They were heading our way, so we got orders to scarper away from the buildings.

At the back of the buildings was an area of vacant ground, no trees, just grass—I suppose about 200–300 yards across—and we all raced out there and lay flat on the ground.

You could hear the planes and could always tell when the bombs were dropped, when the engine note would change. And after a few seconds, you could hear the bombs coming. It is a funny thing about bombs, it is the only thing that you can hear coming towards you. If a bullet goes past you, you can hear it go past…but if it doesn't go past and it hits you, you don't hear it. It is travelling faster than the speed of sound. The same with a shell, you don't hear the one that lands on top of you. A mortar bomb, you will hear it in the last two seconds of its flight, but an aerial bomb—you can hear the damn thing coming all the way, and it is very scary.

We could hear these coming all the way down and we heard the first ones hit several hundred yards south of us, and they were all blanket-bombing of course, which means the area between where the first bomb lands and the second bomb lands is governed by the speed of the plane and how fast they fall out. It's many hundreds of yards and we could hear these explosions coming towards us. We were lying flat on our faces and the blastwave was so great it actually lifted us off the ground a couple of inches. It took about twenty or thirty seconds for all the bombs to fall, and all this time, I kept thinking, "This is it; this is where it finishes."

Then it stopped and the last bomb fell about fifty yards away. Fortunately, the ground was terribly soft, and the only real damage was from the shockwaves. Although one bomb did land off-centre in behind us and two of our blokes were killed and another fellow had his foot blown off.

The next day, we were loaded onto a train and we travelled north-east out of Bangkok to a small town whose name I have never been able to find out. It was probably 150 kilometres out. The country there was open farming country, not particularly given to rice paddies. It looked as though it could have carried cattle or something like that. It was fairly well settled with small villages and farmhouses all scattered around the place.

Our camp was a few kilometres outside the town and a lot of fellows were already there. I suppose the camp was not terribly big. There might have been 300–400 fellows there and it was well set up. The food was quite good actually.

We were getting a reasonable amount to eat, and the Japs weren't all that bad.

# CAVE DIGGING, OR...

——————— ◆ ◇ ◆ ———————

The work we were doing, well, some of the gangs were digging great caves out of the hill which was three or four kilometres away from the camp. What it was for, nobody ever found out, but they were digging three or four of these gigantic caves into this hillside. I found out after we were back home that the Japanese High Command had issued an order that, in early August, all prisoners were to be killed and the bodies were to be buried[42]. That was what the caves were for.

My job, with others, was doing the roadwork leading up to this. We were there for a month or six weeks and one of our fellows died from dysentery and I'd got his blanket. By now I had no hat, a shirt, a lap-lap to cover the bottom part of me, and a pair of Jap sandshoes with toes wired up so they wouldn't flap about. I still had my army pack, mess tin, knife, spoon and a few personal belongings that I had carried with me all the way through, and that was it.

About the middle of May, some 100 of us with a Warrant Officer, Regular Army, Australian in charge of us, we were told to move the following day and marched out with all the equipment from the cookhouses, and the cooks going with us to prepare meals, and all the Jap gear which was on two Japanese wooden carts.

---

[42] There are few surviving copies of the order, issued by the Japanese Imperial Army, 1st August 1944. A translation notes *"In any case, it is the aim not to allow the escape of a single one, to annihilate them all, and not to leave any traces."* Source: http://www.mansell.com/pow_resources/Formosa/doc2701-trans.html

We travelled north and stayed well away from the towns mostly for the first few days; we walked along dirt roads through the scrub country and got onto a railway, and we marched along the railway line dragging these carts with us. Of course, after a couple of days of this, the carts fell apart, so we had to carry what had been on the carts—which was not only our own cooking gear but the Japs' cooking gear as well.

We started marching just after daybreak, just after we had a bit of a feed and we kept going until we had a break at lunchtime—although nothing to eat at lunchtime mainly—and then on until just about dark, until we found a camping site.

It was decided by the Officer then that it was impossible for the cookhouse to get ahead of us and have any sort of meal prepared by the time we reached the campsite. So, it was decided that each group of men, grouping up in threes, would prepare their own meals.

We were issued with a quantity of rice; I don't remember just how much, but it wasn't a hell of a lot, and occasionally some greens, and occasionally some of the dried fish that was pretty common around the place. When we got to the camp in the evening, the three of us had a billycan in which we cooked the rice. You can't cook rice properly in a billy can so we simply stewed it up and boiled it, and added whatever else there was and hoed into it.

We tried to keep some for breakfast because you didn't have much time in the morning to cook your own breakfast, and there wasn't any way you could keep it going through to the midday meal. Rice won't keep once it's been cooked, and it goes off very quickly in the hot climate.

We mostly slept out in the open, usually in a clearing somewhere in the scrub. We got back into some heavy jungle after a while, and mainly onto just a trail through the jungle, with no real road or anything. The going became heavy because the wet season was coming and there was rain and mud everywhere. We were wet most of the time.

We found out that if it rained at night and there was no cover, which there rarely was, the best thing to do was to put your blanket in the pack and simply sleep in the wet because if your blanket got wet, it not only became very heavy to carry, but it took an awful long time to dry out. We did sleep one night, I remember, in a Thai temple. And we slept dry that night, and another night we slept underneath a school.

During the day, we would try and gather up some greens, whatever we could. There was a vegetable that grew wild on the side of the road. It was called Kangkong *(water spinach)* and it tasted just like beans cooked up, and we presumed it had some goodness. We were all getting pretty thin by now because we were actually on the road for three months. At one stage, we had to cross a river—I don't know which one, but it was a wide river, about 300 yards across and with all the rain, it was running like crazy.

Thai boats were to take us across. The one we got on was about the same size as the one where we hold our reunion on ANZAC Day in Sydney. I suppose probably 100 of us were packed all over this damn thing and we didn't think it would ever get across, but the Thais were marvellous boatmen. They got through no problem at all.

If anybody got sick or injured on the march, we carried them.

We made up litters from rice bags and a couple of bamboo poles and took turns to carry them until they got better, or we finished the march.

I got crook one day. Instead of eating kangkong, I ate some other thing that looked similar, but it turned out to be poisonous.[43]

The following morning, I couldn't even stand up, so they carried me that day. But I did my fair share in carrying other fellows, so it was fairly evenly worked out.

I think we probably covered 400-500km on that march.

The one thing that stood out afterwards was the fact that wherever we stopped overnight, there could be a village nearby, nearly always one of the saffron robed monks would be wandering around. They observed us at a distance all the way through. We found out afterwards that the British had them enlisted as secret service agents and they kept a tab on us and they reported to the British where we all were.

Nobody knew where we were going on this march, but my theory was—and the other fellows agreed—that we were going to get lost. Japs didn't want too many prisoners found because they knew the war was going against them and just wanted to get rid of us.

We had to forage every afternoon when we stopped for firewood to cook our meal. I teamed up with Harry Simister and another chap whose name I can't remember. We took turns in cooking the evening meal which meant popping the rice into the billycan, popping the greens or whatever else we had with it and boiling it up, and that was the feed.

---

[43] This may have been Kangkong; it's known to accumulate both parasites as well as cadmium, lead, and mercury. It needs to have the stems cut properly and to be thoroughly boiled to avoid food poisoning (or worse).

We were all starting to get a bit slim by now because the food wasn't real good. The Japs were cranky buggers and they didn't make life any easier for us.

We camped one night outside a village and we were allowed to go off foraging for firewood, and about six of us wandered off together gathering firewood everywhere; the Thais came out and gave us all a bunch of bananas.

We knew this was against the rules. We weren't allowed to accept anything like this and on the way back, the Jap guard found us with our bananas, he lined us all up and went through us one by one with a ruddy great bamboo stick. I finished up with a very sore shoulder and a cut on the back of my head the medical orderly had to put four stitches in afterwards. But funnily enough, we were allowed to keep the bananas. Never could figure the Japs out.

# THE WAR'S END

───── ◆ ◇ ◆ ─────

In late August, we were marching through a small village. I think we were way up in the north somewhere near Chang Mai, and one day the villagers started to call out, "War finish! War Finish!" (*Japan surrendered 2nd September 1945*).

Through the village, we marched on a bit farther and I happened to trip and fall over, out of line. The Jap guard came up and shoved me with his rifle butt and called me to get back in line. I lost my bloody temper and I got up and pushed him.

I said, "Get out, you bloody bastard."

All the boys said, "Oh wacko Lofty, good on you." Fortunately, the war was over—and fortunately for me, the guard knew it. Otherwise, I would be history.

That night, we were marched into a well-built, former Thai Army camp. It was empty, abandoned, but with good well-built wooden huts with wooden platforms to sleep on, and we cooked our meal up and climbed onto the bunks and got a good night's sleep.

I had another good fortune that night.

I woke up early and there was a Jap guard sitting on the foot of my bed asleep. I had great pleasure in putting both my feet on his backside and pushing him hard onto the floor.

The next day, all the Japs disappeared. There was a Thai town not far away and some decent food arrived—not luxurious but fairly good quantities, and we all had a good feed.

The following day, our Warrant Officer worked with the Thai's and loaded us onto a train, in carriages no less, and we set off down south. The Warrant Officer in charge of us was a remarkable bloke. He was regular army and reminded me very much of Reg the way he looked after the men.

I know that after we got back home, we were all interrogated to a degree and every one of us recommended that this bloke should get a medal for the way he looked after everybody. I don't know whether he ever got one or not.

We were on the train for two and a half days and we arrived at a place which had obviously been a Japanese camp because there was an aerodrome nearby. The train stopped at a siding and we all got out, and way up front there was a British Officer, a Major. He must have been about 6'6" tall with a big moustache and we heard afterwards he was from the Royal Marine Commandos. They had been in the country for six months with the Thai monks co-operating with them, and they knew exactly where everybody was and what everybody was doing.

Funny thing was, the Major got hold of the Jap officer who had been in charge of us and they went walking away into the jungle. A short while later, the Major came back.

"Funny thing," he said, "The poor beggar shot himself."

We noticed the Major was carrying an American Colt 45 automatic in his belt.

When we walked into this camp, we found that there were clothes available – shorts, shirts, no boots, but sandshoes, hats and plenty of food. Cooks were there. I don't know where they came from, but they weren't our boys. We stayed there for the best part of a week. We were vaccinated and inoculated, and MO's went through us. I know my vaccination went sour on me and I had a very sore arm for most of the time. Then we got on the train and in another day and a half, we arrived in Bangkok.

On our way down, we had picked up a lot of other POWs, some British, but mostly Australian. When we were at the aerodrome camp, the British flew in a number of Dakota planes (*also known as Douglas C-47 Skytrain*) and took the Brits to India. Arriving in Bangkok, our total number would have been about 500, all Australian.

AUSTRALIAN WAR MEMORIAL                                                    018456

*Figure 27: Douglas C-47 transport plane, New Guinea c. 1945. (AWM 018456)*

# POST-WAR BANGKOK

———— ◆ ◇ ◆ ————

It was most amazing. At Bangkok, we came into the main railway station, a big long one about as vast as Sydney's Central Station, and the whole length of the platform was taken up with tables laden with food. All the officials from Bangkok were there to greet us and we were invited to tuck into this food.

There were cakes, pies, and fruits—and you name it, it was there. We had another feed.

Then were moved on trucks to what we believe was a university building, a very large, well-built stone and brick place surrounded by a very high stone wall and there were quite a lot of fellows who had been brought back in and reassembled there.

There were hundreds of us, probably a thousand, even. There we had further medical exams and plenty of food and stayed there for the best part of a week.

When the Japanese occupied Bangkok in 1941, a lot of the businesses, the shops and whatever, were occupied and run by Chinese. This was pretty common throughout all the far-Eastern cities and the Japanese didn't like the Chinese and vice versa, so they kicked the Chinese out of the shops and gave all the businesses over to the Thais. When the war finished, the Chinese decided they wanted to have their shops back, but the Thais weren't co-operative. So a little bit of a civil war erupted there for a few weeks. The Chinese had a little habit of riding down the street on motor scooters and tossing a hand grenade into one of their former shops.

Another chap and I were walking outside the camp at the university one day, and around the corner came a section of Thai military with a light automatic. They set the automatic up in the middle of the road and started firing off. They weren't firing at us but we were in the line of fire and all of a sudden, we found bullets stitching a path across the rock wall that surrounded the university. We dived for cover into the ditch and crawled our way back inside.

After being occupied for five years, Bangkok was revelling in its freedom. It was a most extraordinary city that never stopped— twenty-four hours a day. The streets were full of people, the shops were full of people, and everybody was happy. Very few motor cars in the city, but a lot of the trishaws—bicycles with the carriages on the back—replaced the rickshaws and motor scooters and bicycles by the million.

These were friendly people, all having a wonderful time and we wandered all over the place. Not much to do in the town apart from siteseeing. There were little bars everywhere but no beer, so we had to drink the local whiskey, which was made somewhere out of town, and pretty rough-looking stuff it was too, but it served the purpose.

# BACK TO SINGAPORE

——————— ◆ ◇ ◆ ———————

We stayed in Bangkok for about a week or ten days, then a team of us was loaded onto a DC3 and flew down to Singapore where there was a camp prepared on the coast not far from where the big guns were, about halfway between Singapore and Changi.

Here were tents and ablution blocks, and there were probably 100 of us there.

We had nothing to do all day but sit around and smoke and drink beer. We got a bottle of Australian beer per person per day, which was very acceptable. And we only had one pair of shorts and a shirt each and a pair of sandshoes and a giggle hat *(a wide-brimmed hat, also called a boonie)*. Every day, usually straight after lunch, we washed the shorts and shirts and wrapped a towel around our waists and put the shorts and shirts out on the tent fly to dry.

AUSTRALIAN WAR MEMORIAL                                          117230

*Figure 28: Admiral Lord Louis Mountbatten GCVO CB DSO*
*Supreme Allied Commander South East Asia, chatting with*
*ex-POWS of the Japanese, Changi, 1945. (AWM 117230)*

I had done this one day, and a jeep drove in, driven by a man with a woman beside him and in the back was the most fierce-looking Gurkha sergeant with a sten gun on his lap. The driver was Lord Louis Mountbatten, the Supreme Commander in this area of the war. He got out and his wife got out, and she walked one way and he walked the other and came around and spoke to everybody. And here we were with nothing on but towels wrapped around our waists and the Supreme Commander was there talking to us.

After about fifteen minutes, he called out, "We must go, we must go, we're late." She took no notice. So, he walked over, picked her up, plonked her on to the seat next to him and climbed aboard and drove off again.

# OFF HOME TO AUSTRALIA

◆ ◇ ◆

A fter about a week in Singapore, about ten of us were picked out, went into town and they loaded us into a Sunderland Flying Boat, and we were on our way home. We flew the first night to Labuan in Eastern Borneo, spent the night there in an Army Field Hospital and the next day flew to Morotai, an island almost due east of there.

I spent another night there in an Army Hospital and the next day flew to Darwin.

AUSTRALIAN WAR MEMORIAL                                                    AC01 26

*Figure 29: Sunderland flying boat, taxiing,
c. 1945. (AWM AC0126)*

We were only to spend a day there so didn't get into the town at all. We were quartered in the Army barracks quite a fair way out of town. The funny thing was that we were kitted out there and given uniforms, and the works. In the Quartermaster's (QM) store, the QM said, "Anything you want, take it." Most extraordinary for the army because in previous quartermasters' stores, getting something out of them was like drawing a tooth. We could have taken anything we wanted: shirts, shorts, socks, you name it. Nobody did—as we couldn't care less.

AUSTRALIAN WAR MEMORIAL                                    NEA0330

*Figure 30: RAAF Consolidated PBY Catalina,*
*Queensland c. 1944. (AWM NEA0330)*

The next day, we were loaded onto a Catalina PBY[44] and flew to Cairns, where we were again quartered in an Army Field Hospital there. Beautiful beds with sheets and everything clean and polished,

---

[44] PBY designates PB for Patrol Bomber and Y is the code assigned to its manufacturer, Consolidated Aircraft.

and after dinner that night, there was a picture show on somewhere in the camp and all the mob went down to this and I stayed behind. The ward sister came in and she said, "Why don't you go with the rest of the fellows and look at the pictures?"

I made some excuse but what I couldn't make her understand was that for something like four years, I had been wholly and completely in the company of other men with absolutely no chance to be alone at any time, or virtually none.

This was probably the first chance I had of being on my own for even an hour or two.

The next day, we climbed onto the Cat and went through to Sydney and landed at Rose Bay. A dinghy took us into the wharf and there were Mavis and my sister Peg. Mavis came flying down the wharf and threw her arms around me, and that was the best day of my life, I reckon.

# EPILOGUE

———— ◆ ◇ ◆ ————

Bill Lowcock discharged from the military on 9th of February 1946. He went on to marry Mavis Walker and they raised a family in Queensland, Australia. Bill and Mavis built the Roselea Hotel in Maroochydore in about 1962 and helped form the local Chamber of Commerce.

It was at a Chamber of Commerce meeting attended by Bill that the name "Sunshine Coast" was devised for marketing the region. There are several other references to Bill and his family in the local paper for the area, the *Sunshine Coast Daily*.

Mavis passed away in 2005. In 2006, Bill passed away at the grand age of eighty-six. They are survived by their children, grandchildren, and an extended family.

Both Bill and Mavis are interred at Kulangoor Lawn Cemetery, Kulangoor, Sunshine Coast, Queensland, Australia. I can think of no more fitting conclusion to Bill's story than the words on his memorial plaque:

William Mackenzie (Bill) Lowcock

24.05.1920 – 28.06.2006

*The quiet achiever.*

AUSTRALIAN WAR MEMORIAL                                                   118876

*Figure 31: Ex-POWS with an Australian flag made from*
*mosquito net, handkerchiefs, and belts. (AWM 118876)*

Made in the USA
Coppell, TX
28 July 2021

59586162R00080